ICONIC CARS

CAR AND DRIVER

filipacchi publishing

Contents

Introduction

Ask any teenage gear-head to sketch their dream car, and chances are the resulting silhouette and performance specs will look and sound a lot like the Chevrolet Corvette.

Only a few domestic cars can claim icon status; the Corvette is one of those rare pieces of Americana, whether we're talking about the 1953 original or today's $105,000, 197-mph ZR1. In six generations, the Corvette has carved its own niche out of our cultural landscape with a breath-stealing blend of feral good looks and shattering horsepower.

It all began in the era of car enthusiasm that dawned after World War II. While America pulled out of a postwar recession, sportscar enthusiasts looked to Europe for fine-handling machinery, mostly from Great Britain, in the form of Jaguars and MGs. None of America's automakers could claim a stake in the sportscar market—and as recession swung to boom times, General Motors executives decided it was time to make a play.

The Corvette grabbed the mantle of greatness with the first contact of pen to paper. From the moment it was conceived in the fertile GM design studios directed by Harley Earl, it heralded a high-water mark for the American car industry. It was the convergence of all the back-story lines that would dominate Detroit for decades: big displacement, awe-inspiring speed, and earthy aggression.

It was a sign of great things to come from General Motors, but in its first iteration, the Corvette championed only its unabashedly American good looks— toothy chrome grille, plump fenders, and all. It was no mechanical miracle. Cobbled together from off-the-shelf Chevrolet pieces and fitted with a fiberglass body to save money, the Vette wasn't built to win the racing day, just a race to the showroom floor. First conceived as a budget sportscar at the price of a family sedan, the production Corvette cost nearly $3,500, or almost twice as much as GM had planned.

The concept car's first public showing came at the 1953 New York Auto Show, wearing the "Corvette" nameplate suggested by a GM advertising manager. Within six months the two-seat sportscar went on sale, and launched an iconic journey into history. Over the decades, and through six generations, the Corvette would conquer its own shortcomings on the track, maturing from its grand-touring bluegrass roots into a ferocious, big-block pavement ripper of the first order. The first-generation boulevardier started to bare some performance fangs in 1955 with the introduction of the big-block Chevy V-8, and in 1956 a new look made its debut, with a comet-bright scoop of white making a hairpin turn across the Vette's doors. Mechanical upgrades came with every passing model year, and the Corvette's confidence on the road and on the track grew—and became a metaphor for GM's rise into a world-beating automaker that grabbed more than 60 percent of all new-vehicle sales in the U.S. in 1960.

By 1962, the Corvette had gained the respect of European peers, but a brand-new model ushered in a timeless shape and riveting performance, axing the old live-axle rear end and revving up big-block power. Even today, the 1963 Corvette is considered the pinnacle of style, with its blistered, aquiline fenders earning it the nickname Sting Ray. The names behind this generation—Mitchell, Shinoda, Arkus-Duntov—own a place in Corvette history through their expressive, earth-shaking creation.

From this peak, the Corvette's road to timelessness would have its speed bumps, some of the "severe tire damage" variety. In 1968, a new Vette emerged, and while it wasn't the stunning equal of the C2, the new "C3" Corvette had its own slippery, exaggerated appeal—while bringing massive horsepower and kitschy features like T-tops to the Summer of Love's going-away party. In 1970, the Vette would see top versions throwing out 460 horsepower, as rated by the manufacturer; however accurate those numbers might have been, the mighty Corvette would fall from them quickly, and wouldn't recover its footing for nearly a decade and a half.

In the 1970s and 1980s, the Vette's V-8 engines atrophied as gas prices spiked in lockstep with fuel-economy standards. The C3 Corvette saw progressive downrating as GM fiddled with hardware to meet strict new emissions standards. Then, tougher crash-safety rules took their toll on the Vette's curves, resulting in some awkward front and rear ends that time would not treat with kid gloves. Down in some years to as few as 165 horsepower on call, the Corvette slunk through the malaise years, stumbling to a finale in 1982 when the only Corvette offered for sale was one with an automatic transmission.

C4 in some circles means explosive power, and true to form, the Corvette that took on that alphanumeric code when it bowed in 1984 blew up over sportscar radar with high expectations. It landed some direct hits, with its dart-like fiberglass body, iconic circular taillamps, and removable roof panel. It missed—and missed widely—with a plasticky cabin crowned by big digital gauges, a harsh and unforgiving ride, and a fuel-economy-minded manual transmission with an electrically locking overdrive system.

Over time, GM would massage out some of the worst offenses, none of which kept the Corvette from hitting new sales records. However, especially in this generation, the Corvette's quality record was a sore point—complete with apocryphal stories about chief engineers and plant managers refusing to talk about running changes, which meant no one knew exactly what went into each Corvette coming from the Bowling Green, Kentucky, plant, or how to fix them. In 1990, all could be forgiven as GM introduced the Corvette ZR-1, a 375-horsepower monster with a real six-speed manual shifter and hellacious acceleration, all for only about twice as much as the stock Vette.

GM's spiral into financial difficulty in the earliy 1990s left the Corvette vulnerable to extinction, and horsepower addicts went on deathwatch. Somehow, despite the headwinds, the Corvette survived to emerge in C5 form, in 1997. Essentially the first all-new Corvette since 1953, this Corvette unknotted all the past prejudices against GM's two-seater, thanks to a marvelous shape, a tightly styled cabin, a completely new aluminum-block engine, and a rear-mounted transmission. This sensational Corvette would go on to revive the Z06 model and keep the name polished while the current, all-new Corvette was being bred behind the scenes.

Today's Corvette, the C6, is undeniably the best ever to roll under the nameplate's crossed flags.

The Vette now kicked out 400 hp—in base form—and offered up high-tech ride controls to add more everyday usability to its speedy portfolio. The increasingly sophisticated shape hid the fact that it shared some running gear with another GM sportscar, the hardtop-convertible Cadillac XLR. Then in 2010, the pinnacle of Corvette performance, of all time, was reached when GM launched the 638-hp, $104,000 Corvette ZR1.

While the Corvette legend grew, another automotive icon delivered the news to enthusiasts from behind the sports-car steering wheel. In 1955, *Sports Car Illustrated* took its place on newsstands, documenting the Vette's early years for fans and followers. The magazine shifted into a higher gear, becoming the American authority on cars by mixing colorful writing, expert analysis, and lush photography. That dramatic acceleration was captured with a name change in 1961, when the magazine traded the SCI name for a new one—*Car and Driver*.

Throughout more than 50 years of existence, both the Corvette and *Car and Driver* have been dedicated to pushing the limits of the sports car's 200-mph-plus speedometer. Both became singular names: the Corvette as the most popular sports car in the world, and Car and Driver as the largest selling monthly car magazine on the planet.

For the first time, the editors of *Car and Driver* have culled the very best of the Corvette's history from our archives. On these pages, you'll see our original stories exactly as readers saw them back in the day, so you can follow history as it was being made, and see how *Car and Driver* has evolved over the years.

Whether it's the first or the umpteenth time you've read these stories, you can relive it all—road tests of hallmark models from Sting Ray to ZR1, Corvette wit and wisdom from our columnists, and behind-the-wheel bravado from our expert testers.

We hope you enjoy it all. And for once, we recommend a leisurely pace.

SPORTS CARS ILLUSTRATED

MAY '56

SCI

ROAD TEST:

Chevrolet

Here the author takes a long, fast turn at 60 mph. Note that the rear dips more than front, giving car an understeer effect. Stiffer shocks and springs on the back end would add stability on bends.

By KARL LUDVIGSEN

CHANCES are that by the time you read this the '56 Corvette will have made a profound impression on the whole sports car world, and after having had one under me for a couple of days I will be the last to be surprised. This very early production model showed a willingness and ability to be driven fast and hard under almost all conditions and demonstrated an even greater potential for competitive use. In my opinion, the Corvette as it stands is fully as much a dual-purpose machine as the

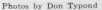
Photos by Don Typond

Although automatically raised and lowered, the top's back window has to be pulled down by hand. This is no problem since the well fitted top clamps down quickly sans fuss.

Cruising at 85, the Corvette produces wind noise over top. However, at such speeds there's bound to be wind disturbance on any car.

Corvette

The Halibrand type knock-offs look like the McCoy, but are actually wheel discs. The real thing is being planned as possible optional equipment.

stock Jaguar, Triumph, or Austin-Healey. Without qualification, General Motors is now building a sports car.

Unfortunately, at this writing accurate information both on the Corvette itself and on their future plans is not available, and the air is rife with rumor. SCI's test car was chassis #1002, and was obtained from the Chevrolet Motor Division through the combined efforts of Shelly Spindel and Alvin Schwartz Chevrolet of Brooklyn, N. Y. Finished in two-tone turquoise with a matching hard top and a white convertible top, it was a real traffic-stopper, and was specifically destined to make a New York TV appearance. As such, it had the full range of options, including white-walls, the hard top, power windows, radio, heater and windshield washer. To our joy it had the close-ratio stick shift, but less happily had the higher, 3.27:1 rear end ratio. It was, all in all, a lot of car and I regret that at this time Chevrolet was not ready to discuss prices. There is little question, though, that it is to be competitive with the Thunderbird.

Now that the "dual-purpose" claim has been made, it should be backed up. Those accustomed to GM products may tend to take the creature comforts for granted, but any owner of an older Corvette will readily testify that those cars could be uninhabitable at times. Much effort has been expended to rectify this, and it has paid off in full.

Entry and exit over the wide sill on the passenger side is easy, for a sports car, but as the driver slides under the steering wheel he becomes aware of one of the car's few major faults. While it is handsome, and provided with more than enough finger ribbing, the wheel is too close to the driver and is non-adjustable. Ex-Jag drivers may find the position natural, but I personally felt that more arm room would be useful, particularly for competition. You also sit close enough to the door for the integral arm rest to be in the way.

The seats themselves are very handsome, and very deceptive. They look like a true bucket type, and the seat bottoms are comfortable enough, but the backs are bolt upright and provide no lateral support for the torso. Adjustment of rake and a more definite "bucket" would improve

them greatly and would obviate a certain amount of fatigue that now occurs. Fore-and-aft adjustment is not extensive, there being just enough room for a six-footer. Leg room is excellent; the left foot can roam about under the suspended pedals, and the brake and throttle are well-placed for heel-and-toe downshifting.

Headroom is also at the bare minimum for six feet of height, with slightly more room under the soft top. In general, the Corvette has very little interior room for such a large car, and it seems that neither GM nor Ford have yet completely solved the sports car seating problem.

Driving the Corvette with the top down is very pleasant, the windshield giving good protection to the top and side. You sit high enough to rest your elbow comfortably on the door, if so inclined. The power windows are handy and reliable, but the power-operated top qualifies as the most fascinating mechanism I have seen on any car. The lid rises, the top emerges, and the lid closes again as the control button is pressed. You must then pull down and clamp the back window section by hand, and close two front latches. It's all very easy, and the finished product is attractive and tight. It can be stowed away just as simply.

The hard top is also easy to install, having two clamps at the front and three bolts and two locating dowels at the rear. It is well finished and padded, and provides unobstructed vision. Light and easy to transport, the top's main fault is arbitrary sealing at the sides of the rear deck.

Instrument panel layout is identical to last year's cars, and has many of the same faults. All the secondary instruments, including the tachometer, are very difficult to read

SPORTS CARS ILLUSTRATED

MAY '56

Twin four-barrel carburetors squat on power plant ready to help deliver 225 bhp at 5200 rpm. At low speeds, only rear carburetor functions. BELOW—Hood raises from rear, reducing possible lifting at high speed. Engine compartment is more accessible for shop work.

A lack of bumpers at the rear will make any Corvette driver over-cautious when backing. Exhaust tubes are in for abuse.

SPECIFICATIONS
CHEVROLET CORVETTE

ENGINE

Cylinders	V8
Bore and stroke	3.75 in x 3.00 in (95 mm x 76 mm)
Displacement	265 cu in (4340 cc)
Compression ration	9.25:1
Max. horsepower	225 bhp @ 5200 rpm
Max. torque	270 lb ft @ 3600 rpm
Max. b.m.e.p.	154 psi

CHASSIS

Wheelbase	102 in
Front track	57 in
Rear track	59 in
Curb weight	2980 lbs
Front/rear distribution	52/48
Test weight	3250 lbs
Turns lock to lock	3.6

Gear ratios:

Gear	Standard	Optional
3rd	3.55	3.27
2nd	4.65	4.28
1st	7.84	7.22
Rev	7.84	7.22

Tire size	6.70 x 15
Brake lining area	158.0 sq in
Fuel capacity	17 gal

PERFORMANCE

TEST CONDITIONS

40°F, light wind, dry concrete surface at sea level.

SPEEDS IN GEARS

Gear	True mph	(Car) mph
1st	64	(60)
2nd	108	(102)
3rd	118.5	(110)
Best run	120.0	

ACCELERATION

Range	Time, Seconds	Gears Used
0-30	3.4	1st
0-40	4.6	"
0-50	6.0	"
0-60	7.5	"
0-70	10.0	1st, 2nd
0-80	12.5	" "
0-90	15.8	" "
0-100	19.3	" "
50-70	4.5	2nd
50-70	5.8	3rd
60-80	4.7	2nd
60-80	7.0	3rd
Standing ¼ mile	15.9	1st, 2nd
Speed at end of quarter	91 mph	

FUEL CONSUMPTION

Hard driving	12 mpg (tank mileage)

26

Instruments are well balanced for eye-appeal, but not practical. Reading them at any speed over forty is difficult. Note simple design of steering wheel.

View shows sleekness of new Corvette. Except for phony air-scoops and knock-off type discs, the car is functional in design.

Small luggage compartment makes long trips restrictive. Jack fits inside spare to conserve space. Larger trunk would destroy line, increase weight.

Fully automatic, the top slips out of the well after the lid raises. Convenience of automation makes added weight of unit bearable.

Corvette interior is well appointed, with leg room for the six-footers. Wrap-around windshield makes getting in and out a bit awkward.

at the bottom of the dash, even if you can take your eyes from the road long enough to find them. The speedometer is well-placed, but quick correlation between the numerals and the divisions is impossible, as they are on different planes. Dial lighting is very good, with rheostat control, and the interior lights are perfect for rallying, being placed under the cowl.

Other interior shortcomings are the dearth of storage space, save for the between-seat compartment, and a conflict between the heater and the passenger's feet. The view forward is very impressive, and clever psychologically. The hood bulges, long fender lines, and cowl vents (which, incidentally, can easily be made functional for dry climates) combine to give an impression of great forcefulness. Vision over this snout is adequate, but not outstanding. The heater and defroster are well up to their jobs,

and the only other irritant might be a very awkward and stiff interior door control.

In spite of numerous open car details, the passengers can be kept warm and dry, and can set their own climate at a literal touch of a button. I can imagine no greater contrast than between this and the forced exposure of the gutty old J2 Cadillac Allard, but the fact is that such an Allard in stock trim would be left behind at the quarter by this incredible Corvette! The figures speak eloquently for themselves, and with the lower 3.55:1 ratio things should happen even more rapidly. As a matter of fact, our speedometer was so very slow that it probably was geared for use with that ratio. Also, the engine was nothing like wound out at the top end, and the lower gearing would probably improve top speed by five to seven miles per hour.

(Continued on page 55)

SCI Road Test: Corvette

(Continued from page 27)

Precision balancing after assembly may have accounted for the clean, smooth running of the engine, and its ability to rev freely to around 5500. For about the first half inch of throttle travel only the rear one of the two four-barrel carburetors is working to prevent overcarburetion at low speeds. When the front quad cuts in the previously unobtrusive exhaust note sharpens and the car starts to move. When backing off at higher speeds there is a not unappealing rap from the duals. Idling is at 1000 rpm when the automatic choke is working and 600 rpm when warm, and the power-plant is tractable enough to lug down to a 12 mph in high.

Featuring special cooling and nine coils instead of the old diaphragm spring, the clutch took a lot of punishment without complaint. It is not easy to get a potent car off the mark with such very high gearing, and this component took the brunt of the effort without signs of heating or slippage. The gearbox wins similar praise for its well-chosen ratios and effective synchromesh. Shifting linkage is smooth and direct, the heavy-knobbed lever being spring-loaded to the right-hand side of the conventional "H" pattern. The synchro can be beaten by a very quick move from first to second, but the movement between the two top gears is impeccable. Synchromesh on low would be a useful boon, but a noiseless downshift can be made by double-clutching.

Due to the high ratios, the standard-shift Corvette is not really at home in town, and Powerglide might be better for. urban use. Out on the road, though, as second gear takes over from first at around sixty and keeps the seat in your back 'til over a hundred, you learn what this car was made for. Cruising is effortless at 85 or 90, though with enough wind noise over the soft top to render the radio unintelligible.

It is in the handling department in particular that the Corvette proves itself the only true American production sports car. The steering is far from perfect but it is fast enough to allow right angles to be taken without removing the hands from the wheel, and this virtue will make up for many vices. The latter include an inch and a half of play, beyond which a strong caster action gives the wheel a springy feel. This little "no-man's-land" in the middle causes some trepidation in tight spots. Once the wheel has been set for a bend, and the car has assumed an initial roll angle, the steering and throttle response are fast and consistent enough to allow very precise control.

Like most American cars this Chevrolet is a very strong understeerer, and requires a lot of helm to keep it on line in a bend. The stock rear end damping is a little weak; too much so to make a full-blooded drift a stable proposition. Cornering speeds and behavior were markedly improved by tire pressure five psi higher than the standard of 25 psi front and 27 psi rear. Raised pressures plus stiffer rear shocks could combine with an already broad track, good weight distribution, and low center of gravity to make the Corvette a real fiend on corners. These criticisms, it will be noted, are minor, and apply equally to many imported machines.

Of course, tire squeal is not entirely absent during these high-speed direction changes, but the car stays in the corner so there can be no real complaints. The Corvette is at its best on a winding open road, and, like the Jaguar, is dramatic but uncomfortable on a twisty back lane. The test car would have been much handier there if the driver had had more arm room and the optional seat belts. He tends to be thrown around more than necessary, but is not as conscious of the car's roll angle as is the passenger.

Brakes are still by far the. weakest link, and it must be admitted that they faded almost into oblivion during the performance tests. They recovered very quickly, though, and pulled the heavy car up with a minimum of slewing even when very hot. I sincerely feel that the substitution of harder Moraine linings or some of the foreign competition brands will improve high-temperature durability and perhaps modify the present spongy feel of the pedal. No power booster was fitted, and required pedal pressure was on the high side.

Very sensibly for a high speed car, the hood is hinged from the front, and opens well out of the way. The battery and brake master cylinder are easy to reach, and the small air cleaners ease access to the engine as a whole. Most awkward feature is the shielding for the ignition wiring, necessary to eliminate radio interference in a Fiber-glas body. Wingnuts quickly free these shields and bare the double-breaker distributor and all but the two left front spark plugs, which are tucked in behind the steering box.

The hydraulic system for the top mechanism is powered by a separate electric motor, which allows operation with the engine off and avoids direct absorption of any engine power. Individual motors operate the door windows.

Well finished and fitted, the trunk is usefully large for a sports car. All luggage must be removed to extricate the spare from its wooden-lidded compartment, which also houses the jack. One carrying feature of many imports that is missed in the Corvette is that handy space right behind the seats for coats, hats, lunches and other items that you don't want to store in the trunk. In the Corvette you either live with them or lock them away.

In almost every respect, the 1956 Corvette is a very satisfying car on the highway, and supplements astonishing performance with a high level of road-holding. Even as it stands, power equipment and all, it has become a serious competitor for Jaguar in Production Class C, and this is by no means General Motors' highest goal. In international events this year the car will be equipped with an optional cam providing 250 bhp at the sacrifice of present low-end smoothness. Also on the fire for either this or next year are engine boosts to 275 bhp, extensive use of light alloy in both body and chassis, and the development of suitable disc brakes by GM's Moraine Division.

It seems likely that the standard Corvettes will remain much as they are, with work on the competition versions proceeding simultaneously as has been the case with Jaguar and their C and D models. Another two or three years could probably see a racing Corvette with as many standard parts as the D retains from the Jaguar line, shrouded in advanced coupe bodywork. GM will learn an incalculable amount from these cars, much of which will be passed on to the standard Corvette and to the passenger car. They've already learned quite a lot, as a matter of fact, most of which shows up in the all-around excellence of the 1956 Corvette.   #

Tiger in a Tuxedo!

The Corvette above is a very civilized vehicle—and hides its secret well. Cruising along the boulevards, whispering past the glitter of café lights, it drifts like a well-mannered dream. It is the epitome of luxury, sweetly sprung, hush-voiced, deep-cushioned, endowed with every convenience artful craftsmen can devise.

But a good many people have discovered to their very genuine surprise that this suave elegance conceals a savage competence. For this is a *sports car*, in the accurate meaning of the term. It is a perfectly docile (and perfectly delightful) town car and touring car. But it also can erupt, instantly, into a full-bore competition car.

Our British cousins and Continental friends have become painfully aware of this—at Pebble Beach, Elkhart Lake, Seattle Seafair, Palm Springs and other sports car gatherings. You can understand their surprise; after all, you don't expect to find a tiger under a tuxedo. But that is the Corvette's unique contribution to motoring—a perfectly harmonious blend of ultimate luxury and blazing road*ability*, all in one polished instrument.

There's never been a combination like this—and you can savor it for yourself at your Chevrolet dealer's. . . . Chevrolet Division of General Motors, Detroit 2, Michigan.

by Chevrolet

SCI

ROAD
TEST:

THE '58 CORVETTE

18

TO mark the fourth birthday of the Corvette, its proud parents, the Chevrolet Motor Division, have announced the 1958 model which has undergone some extensive but not too important changes on the surface and a few rather interesting ones underneath. Starting right at the plastic body, the use of aluminum reinforcements in the cowl structure, inaugurated in mid-'57, has been extended to include the so-called "rocker panels" under the door openings. Bumpers are now bracketed to the frame in conventional American style, relieving the front and rear body panels of loads that are not rightfully theirs. These two items raise the weight "less than 100 pounds", but for racing, most of it can be unbolted and left in the pits without the SCCA batting an eye.

Uncowled dual headlights show how attractive most American front ends would be if we'd get off this "I'm longer than you are" kick. Just below them are really large holes for blasting fresh air onto the brakes, but on our test car, alas, the "holes" were painted black! More on this later on.

Further production experience with the F.I. nozzles and metering controls permits closer control over the air-fuel ratio this year. The warm-up diaphragm is now more sensitive and the air filter is also changed. On all Corvettes, the generator is now on the right-hand side so that the fan-belt engages the water pump pulley over a far greater arc, reducing slippage at high revs. Common to all '58 Chevy's with the 283 cubic incher are a new distributor rotor and a cap with longer sides to help keep out moisture.

Like most manufacturers, Chevrolet is none too happy about some of the attempts made to bring "boulevard" engines up to all-out F.I. specs. More is required than just a

Centrally located, the tachometer may now be readily observed, though it suffers from unwanted reflections off the curved lens, as do the other instruments.

The trunk space shows the American influence on sports car design; observes the Technical Editor, it's huge.

The cornering of the "boulevard" Corvette cannot be described as flat, but to the driver it certainly feels very secure.

The louvers in the hood aren't real but everything underneath it is, and in a very big way.

Duntov high-lift cam and a handful of solid lifters, although the factory is not too specific as to what is. What they have done is clarify the picture of available options.

First of all, here is what an absolutely standard Corvette would have (later we will get into what else can be ordered on the car at the time of purchase): The 283 cubic inch V-8 with a normal camshaft and hydraulic tappets (limiting revs to about 5500, as on our test car), a single four barrel Carter carburetor (#3744925), the "close-ratio" three-speed transmission (also used on other Chevy's with the 283 inch engine), a 3.70/1 ring and pinion, 6.70x15 tires (tubeless

19

15

Fitted with prototype linings, the brakes stood up to SCI's severe brake test very well indeed, considering that full-size wheel discs were worn during the test.

Accessibility of the fuel injection "box of tricks" is really great. There are lots of little bits and pieces but unlike carbs, here they're on the outside.

or not, to choice) on 5Kx15 disc wheels, and a choice of either the hardtop or the hand-operated folding one.

Options available that do not change the basic car's essentially boulevard character include: Powerglide transmission and with it, a 3.55 rear end; electric window equipment (which is no lighter than the hand-operated kind as reported elsewhere) ; a hydraulic mechanism for the folding top; and for the belt-and-suspenders types, both the hard and soft tops may be ordered on one car.

To improve performance, one can order either two Carter quads or fuel injection (we had the latter), the manifolds differing slightly between Powerglide and stick-shift cars. But for the most in "go", there is the 290 bhp @ 6200 rpm "D" fuel injection engine which features a 10.5/1 compression ratio, the high-lift cam, solid lifters, an air intake extension to bring in cool outside air, a reputedly "more efficient radiator", and a tachometer reading up to 8000 rpm. Especially designed for this engine, but definitely available on its own, as on our test car, is a really delightful, all-synchronized, four-speed gearbox.

In much the same category are the Positraction limited-slip differentials available with either the 3.70, 4.11, or the 4.56 ratios (and though you can't order it this way, the normal Chevy 3.89 gears will fit the carriers of either the 4.11 or the 4.56 Positraction diffs). To give slightly better side-load characteristics, wider (5½Kx15) rims are available for fitting 7.10 or 7.60x15 tires, racing or otherwise; the difference between the two enabling last minute "gear" swaps to be made at races.

For the guy who is really serious about his racing, a heavy-duty brake and suspension package is offered in an all or nothing deal. To get this package, you must also order the "D" engine and the Positraction differential. But what a package! Stiffer front coils give a spring rate 13½% higher.

The anti-roll bar is 40% stiffer. The rear springs, with an extra leaf, have a 9½% higher rate. The shock absorbers, with 88% larger working area, have different valving and finally, the steering ratio is changed from 21/1 to 16.3/1 by lengthening the third arm idler.

The famous Cerametallic brakes are fitted and it is interesting to note that although the drum diameter remains at eleven inches and the shoes are a full half inch wider, the total braking area is actually reduced 20%, because the forward shoes are lined over only half their length. To reduce the amount of braking done by the rear wheels, the brake cylinders there are only 0.875 inch diameter instead of one inch, whereas the front ones remain at 1.125. The drums have cooling fins cast on the rim, and as a further option, vented backing plates with air scoops are available. Those large holes up front that we mentioned before may then be opened up and a duct will carry air back, not just to the front brakes, but under the door sills all the way to the rear ones, too.

The Cerametallic brakes are definitely not intended for all types of driving. Corvettes so equipped are delivered to the customer with a placard on the windshield which reads, "This car is not for street use". Until warmed up, they are quite apt to pull strongly to one side or the other; not just the thing for Grandma on her jaunts to the grocery store!

Faced with the realities of the American scene, Chevrolet now follows tradition in marketing two apparently similar, yet actually quite different sports cars, one for the every day sort of user who might occasionally go racing, and another for the serious competitor in the Production category. However, in this case, the engine mods from the racing model are readily available without the HD brake and suspension kit, which may seem rather the wrong way around. But at least you can't get the "D" engine with the

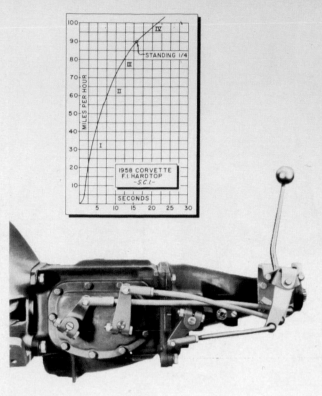

One of the Corvette's secrets of success is this really splendid 4-speed all-synchromesh gearbox.

1958 CHEVROLET CORVETTE F.I. HARDTOP

PERFORMANCE

TOP SPEED:

Est. 125 mph .... (see text)

ACCELERATION:

From zero to

30 mph	.... 3.3 sec.	80 mph	.... 12.2
40 mph	.... 4.5	90 mph	.... 15.7
50 mph	.... 5.8	100 mph	.... 21.4
60 mph	.... 7.6	Standing ¼ mile	.... 15.7
70 mph	.... 9.5	Speed at end of quarter ... 90 mph	

SPEED RANGES IN GEARS:

Corresponding to 750-5500 rpm

I	.... 0-56 mph	III	 13-93
II	 10-72	IV	.... 17-top

FUEL CONSUMPTION:

	Test Car	Competition
Racing	.... 15 mpg	est. 8 mpg
Average driving (under 60 mph)	.. 18.5 mpg	

BRAKING EFFICIENCY:

(12 successive emergency stops from 60 mph, just short of locking wheels):

1st stop	 60	
2nd	 60	
3rd	 63	
4th	 63	
5th	 59	(rear wheel locked momentarily)
6th	 63	
7th	 63	
8th	 60	
9th	 59	(rear wheel locked momentarily)
10th	 62	
11th	 59	
12th	 54	

SPECIFICATIONS

POWER UNIT:

Type	.... V-8
Valve Arrangement	.... Pushrod, in-line ohv
Bore & Stroke	.... 3.875 x 3.00 in (98.4 x 76.2 mm)
Stroke/Bore Ratio	.... 0.774/1
Displacement	.... 283 cu in (4640 cc)
Compression Ratio	.... 9.5/1 (10.5/1 with optional camshaft)
Carburetion by	.... Rochester constant flow fuel injection (one or two Carter quads optional)
Max. Power	.... 250 bhp @ 5000 rpm
Max. Torque	.... 305 lb-ft @ 3800 rpm
Idle Speed	.... 750 rpm

DRIVE TRAIN:

Transmission ratios		Test Car	Optional
Stick shift:	I	.... 2.20	2.21 (non-synchro)
	II	.... 1.66	1.32
	III	.... 1.31	1.00
	IV	.... 1.00	
	Rev.	.... 2.25	2.21
Powerglide Low		3.82-1.82	
High		1.82-1.00	
Rev.		1.82	

Final drive ratio (test car) ..... 3.70 (hypoid)
Other available final drive ratios . 3.55 (std for Powerglide), 4.11, 4.56
Limited slip "Positraction" differential available with the 3.70, 4.11, and 4.56 ratios.
Axle torque taken by .... Leaf springs

CHASSIS:

Wheelbase	.. 102 in
Front Tread	.. 57 in
Rear Tread	.. 59 in
Suspension, front	.. Unitized, independent, unequal length wishbones, coil springs, 11/16″ dia anti-roll bar (13/16″ optional)
Suspension, rear	.. Semi-elliptic leaf springs
Shock absorbers	.. Tubular hydraulic, 1″ piston diameter (1⅜″ optional)
Steering type	.. Semi-reversible, recirculating ball, center-point linkage
Steering wheel turns L to L	..... 3.7
Turning diameter	.. 38½ ft right, 39 ft left
Brake lining area	.. 157 sq in (121 sq in optional—see text)
Tire size	.. 6.70 x 15 (7.10/7.60 x 15 optional)
Rim size	.. 5K x 15 (5½K x 15 optional)

GENERAL:

Length	.... 177 in
Width	.... 73 in
Height	.... 51 in
Ground clearance	.... 6 in
Curb weight, factory data	...... 2912 lbs
Weight distribution, F/R	...... 52½/47½
Fuel capacity	.... 16.4 U.S. gallons

RATING FACTORS:

	Test Car	Competition model with 4.11/1 gears and 7.10 x 15 tires
Bhp per cu in	.... 0.88	1.02
Bhp per sq in piston area	.... 2.65	3.07
Torque lb-ft per cu in	.... 1.08	1.02
Pounds per bhp	...... 11.6	est. 10.3
Piston speed @ 60 mph	.. 1420 fpm	1550 fpm
Piston speed @ max bhp	.. 2500 fpm	3100 fpm
Brake lining area per ton	.. 108 sq in/ton	83 sq in/ton
Speed in IVth gear @ 1000 rpm	.. 21.4 mph	19.4 mph

Powerglide transmission! That *would* be too much!

One of the pleasanter aspects of this test was that, being in the nature of a sneak preview, the entire operation was conducted on GM's Proving Grounds at Warren, Michigan. After the brake fade and acceleration tests were completed on a 1½ mile level straight, we turned the Corvette loose on a sample road circuit that rather resembled Torrey Pines with its multiplicity of turns of varying radius, camber, and even surface texture. A visitor is said to have remarked naively that GM, with all its money, certainly could have afforded to build better roads than these. Be that as it may, we were able, in a very short time, to discover how the '58 Corvette behaves in nearly every conceivable road situation. Briefly, it may be summed up as "very well indeed."

There are no tricks at all to the steering, which is amazingly light at all times. We went through a series of ess-bends at speeds ranging from 40 to 70 mph. The only time the car felt at all uncertain was on a special piece of pavement featuring ridges running parallel to our direction of travel. The reaction here was pretty typical, the back end wanted to walk out somewhat when we crossed them on a diagonal. Elsewhere on the track, when we abruptly crested a sharp rise in the middle of a seventy miles an hour bend, the front of the car moved out only slightly, a tribute to a well-arranged front suspension and the high polar moment of inertia. On really tight hairpins, tighter ones than you have any right to be going that fast on, the steering is still light, though the steering lock seems to call for rubber arms. (The HD kit reduces the 3.7 turns lock to lock to under 3.)

Whether on fast bends or slow, when you reach the limits of adhesion, the back starts to come around in a calm, unhurried manner that leaves you plenty of time to get off

(Continued on page 50)

'58 Corvette

(Continued from page 21)

the throttle a bit. On a really rough surface, the manner would be rather less unruffled, for the rear axle assembly is a heavy item of unsprung weight. After finishing the tests, we were told that the car we had been driving had not a one of the HD suspension options. We were suitably impressed.

The fact that acceleration times for this car differ somewhat from those of our previous Corvette tests is more likely due to the easy-going driving technique used than anything else. Our test driver, Mr. Rose, who was provided by GM to do the driving while the Technical Editor did the timing, confessed that standing starts were not his specialty. As we have said before, they were not the Corvette's most polished maneuver either. It is a crying shame that the new "four-link" rear suspension on the regular Chevy's is not used here, where its ability to completely eliminate axle wind-up would be most appreciated. Parenthetically, this major advance in rear suspension (for American cars, that is) comes about as an incidental result of the switch to air suspension and the attendant loss of a means of location (provided formerly by the leaf springs).

Once under way, the Positraction differential really earns its keep and the acceleration is quite breath-taking. The gear ratios in the four speed gearbox (at last!) are marvelously spaced — the ratio step between gears ranges from 1.265 to 1.325— and *all* gears are synchronized (will wonders never cease?). It is at least the equal of any gear box we've ever tried, not only with respect to the suitability of the ratios to the engine performance, but the smoothness of the synchromesh brings to mind the old metaphor about a hot knife and butter.

One fault which did show up toward the end of our acceleration runs was a trace of clutch slip when rushing the shift. When you consider that for the previous ten days this same car had been subjected to the machinations of various and sundry road-testing "experts" from all sorts of publications, then this is perhaps understandable.

Because our tests were made on a regular working day at the Proving Grounds, the normal "traffic" on the high speed straight (2½ miles of level, three-lane road in each direction with a banked turnaround at each end) prevented the Test Manager, Mr. Caswell, from allowing us to exceed 110 mph. With the same final drive ratio and engine as last year's F.I. test car, the top speed should be about the same, namely 125 mph, as the frontal aspect is not changed all that much.

As before, the throttle linkage seems a bit quicker than we would prefer, and with the faster bends requiring careful feathering, it is necessary to brace the edge of your right foot against the transmission bulge, pivoting it from there to

(Continued on page 52)

'58 Corvette

(Continued from page 51)

operate the throttle. The steering wheel, in typical Chevrolet fashion, is right under the driver's chin. Even so, the Corvette is very easily controlled, the brake and clutch pedals are both well placed and smooth in operation, and there is puhlenty of room to stretch your left foot — or brace it, on sharp right turns. And brace it you must, because the Corvette's bucket-style seats are the best argument for seat belts we've seen. At the risk of repeating last year's criticisms all over again, you sit *on* them, not *in* them, and there is virtually no lateral support whatsoever. Seat belts will be standard equipment this year, which is admirable indeed; but better contoured seats would be another big step ahead, too.

The brakes were so good that we kept up our punishing test for twelve stops instead of the usual ten, and it was only in the last two that a slight but definite weakening showed up. We were therefore quite disappointed to find that these were experimental linings only. Still, it's encouraging, as it shows that Chevrolet's been doing a lot of work to provide the average Joe with significantly better brakes, without his being subjected to the drawbacks of the HD kit's Cerametallics — and with a fair amount of success.

For the price of the Corvette, check with your Chevrolet dealer; GM says they're all independent businessmen who are free to set their own prices. Especially on the options, we might add. Without quoting any figures, we'd say that on the basis of local (N.Y.) prices the Corvette ranks as a Best Buy, both as a boulevard sports car and as a competition model.

Stephen F. Wilder

MG Record Run

(Continued from page 23)

this car. You sit in the nose and have no view of the car at all. When I drifted away from the black line once, the car squirmed a few times on the damp salt and the feeling was as though you were sitting on a platform six feet ahead of the front wheels, with the car wagging behind you."

Moss' comments after his official record runs were cool and casual. "It's the fastest I've ever driven," he said, "but it really was a pleasant, uneventful ride. When accelerating, even in third gear I had to be careful to avoid snaking. You're not really in control in this sort of car . . . you just sort of guide it along. Gyroscopic wheel hop is pronounced at these speeds and you musn't fight the wheel; a light touch is OK, but to grip the wheel is to get into trouble. Steering a car like this is like keeping your balance while walking on a railroad rail — not terribly difficult, just tricky."

MG's decision to build the EX 181

(Continued on page 53)

Mr. Corvette and His Cars

By Jan P. Norbye

Zora Arkus-Duntov is so firmly identified with Corvettes they could bear his name

With the original Sting Ray and the Corvette Sting Ray sport coupé in the background, C/D's tech editor (left) discusses Corvette development with Duntov.

After ten years of Corvette production, with constant improvement year by year, it is a pleasure to report that the 1963 car (October C/D) represents a major advance on its predecessors. It is the most radically redesigned Corvette since the inception of that model name, and many of the changes were derived from a number of experimental Chevrolets, some of which were raced extensively. Great credit is due to Chevrolet's engineering development program and to the one man who sparked that program and made the new Corvette possible—Zora Arkus-Duntov, Mr. Corvette.

Paradoxically, Duntov was not connected with the design of the original Corvette. He joined Chevrolet Engineering when Maurice Olley, the suspension expert who served as a consultant on many GM experimental programs, was engaged on "Project Opel," the open two-seater which became the first Corvette. Duntov was later appointed Director of High Performance Vehicle Design and Development, with responsibility for the technical development of the Corvette as his primary duty, but also for special engine and chassis projects on other Chevrolet models.

The industry knew there was a market for an American sports car as early as 1950, and interest was sparked by such efforts as the Willys Jeepster, the fiberglass-bodied Kaiser-Darrin two-seater and the Lincoln-based Muntz Jet. While Olley was on "Project Opel," rumors reached GM that Ford was working on a similar car to be called the Thunderbird. The Corvette prototype was built in near-record time, by using standard components of proved reliability wherever possible, and America's first postwar sports car was born.

A wheelbase of 102 inches was chosen because the successful Jaguar XK-120 had that wheelbase, and several other dimensions in the first Corvette, such as seating, were deliberately identical to those of the Jaguar.

The Corvette frame was a cross-braced channel-section structure, and the engine was a three-carburetor version of the familiar Chevrolet Six tuned to develop 150 bhp at 4,200 rpm. The wishbones-and-coil spring front suspension used many standard parts, but had a heavier anti-roll bar, and the rigid rear axle was carried on semi-elliptic leaf springs.

The prototype had a fiberglass body, but a steel body was to be used in production. However, a pilot series was made with fiberglass bodies, and on the basis of their trouble-free operation it was decided to drop the steel

The original Corvette of 1953 had a six-cylinder single-carb engine, Powerglide automatic transmission and fiberglass body.

Chevrolet built the original Corvair as a GM Motorama dream car in 1955, using a Corvette chassis for this fastback coupé.

The body was restyled for 1956, the V-8 engine became available and then its competition potential first became apparent.

The 1960 Corvette was available with a rich choice of racing equipment, based on experience with the Corvette SS of 1957.

CONTINUED 41

CORVETTE CONTINUED

body. The least typically sports-car feature of the first Corvette was the automatic transmission, a modified Powerglide. It was not until 1955 that the three-speed close-ratio stick shift became available. This was followed by the excellent four-speed all-synchromesh unit two years later.

Zora Duntov spent most of 1956 perfecting Chevrolet's Rochester port-type fuel injection, and was also charged with setting up a factory team for Sebring the following year, with experimental Corvettes. The result was the Corvette SS, a most promising design which was killed by the AMA resolution on racing (and speed and performance advertising) after a single, not very successful racing appearance.

Its engine was a tuned 283-cube Chevrolet V-8 with aluminum cylinder heads and Rochester constant-flow fuel injection, developing 310 bhp. A close-ratio four-speed gearbox was coupled to a quick-change Halibrand rear end suspended in the specially made space frame. Rear suspension was by a de Dion tube, four radius rods, and sharply splayed coil springs with concentric telescopic shock absorbers. Inboard drum brakes were used at the rear, normal drums mounted on the front wheels.

In addition to the team cars, an extra practice car had been built, which was to have its own history. It was transformed at GM Styling, where it was furnished with a new body designed by Bill Mitchell (and renamed the Sting Ray). Later it received a series of chassis improvements. In cooperation with Duntov and Chevrolet Engineering, it was prepared for Dick Thompson to race. In contrast to the Corvette SS, it did very well, and after test-driving it recently in its latest form, with a 327-cube V-8, Dunlop disc brakes and a locked differential, we feel that it would be competitive in big-league sports-car racing today. .

The Corvette SS and the Sting Ray have had a considerable influence on the design of the 1963 Corvettes, although the de Dion rear end and the tubular space frame have not been carried over to the new model. The rear suspension of the Corvette Sting Ray is based on that of another Chevrolet experimental car—the open-wheel single-seater designated CERV-1. This car, of course, was also a creation of Zora Arkus-Duntov.

With only the engine and transmission remaining from the standard Corvette, the 1963 models can be called all-new, yet they have many well-proved components. Not many manufacturers are in a position to achieve such combinations, and certainly 10 years ago Chevrolet knew less about sports cars and racing than,

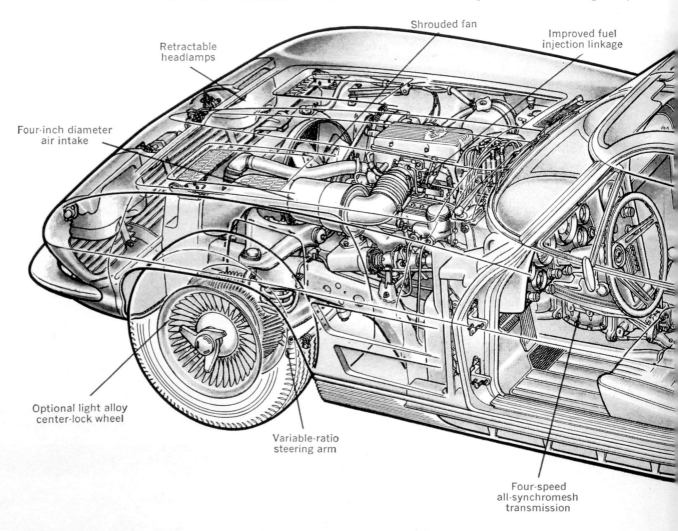

Shrouded fan

Improved fuel injection linkage

Retractable headlamps

Four-inch diameter air intake

Optional light alloy center-lock wheel

Variable-ratio steering arm

Four-speed all-synchromesh transmission

for instance, Chrysler. The long-term research and development instituted by Duntov in his first years at Chevrolet is paying off handsomely today.

To return to the CERV-1, its development differed from both the SS and the Sting Ray. In 1958, Duntov was seriously thinking of redesigning the Corvette as a rear-engined car. There were various reasons why the rear-engined two-seater was never built. Surprisingly, the most important single cause for the project being abandoned was the poor view from the driver's seat, caused by a low seating position and big front wheels. But the rear-engined ideas had matured by late 1960, when the single-seater was first shown publicly. In this design, a fully independent rear suspension had been judged superior to a de Dion layout, and the resultant system has been copied on the Corvette Sting Ray (but a transverse leaf spring has replaced the splayed coils of the CERV-1). One reason for the change in the springs lies in the fact that the 1963 Corvette is a much heavier car. If coil springs were to be used, they would have to be of larger diameter. Problems of finding space would then inevitably present themselves, especially with the production car's outboard brakes. It would have been possible to relocate the springs, but the leaf spring provides a fully acceptable solution.

Duntov's experimental cars have placed Chevrolet

CORVETTE STING RAY SPORT COUPÉ

ENGINE:

Displacement	327 cu in, 5,370 cc
Dimensions	8 cyl, 4.00-in bore, 3.25-in stroke
Valve gear	Pushrod-operated overhead valves
Compression ratio	11.25 to one
Power (SAE)	360 bhp @ 6,000 rpm
Torque	352 lb-ft @ 4,000 rpm
Carburetion	Rochester fuel injection

DRIVE TRAIN:

Clutch............Borg & Beck 10-in single dry plate

Gear	Synchro	Ratio	Step	Overall	Mph per 1,000 rpm
Rev	No	2.26	—	—.36	—9.5
1st	Yes	2.20	33%	8.14	9.7
2nd	Yes	1.64	27%	6.15	12.9
3rd	Yes	1.31	51%	4.84	16.3
4th	Yes	1.00		3.70	21.4

Final drive ratio: 3.70 to one (3.08, 3.36, 3.55, 3.70, 4.11 and 4.56 available with Positraction).

CHASSIS:

Wheelbase	98 in
Track	F 56.3 in, R 57.0 in
Length	175.3 in
Tire size	6.70 x 15 (4-ply)
Curb weight	3,015 lbs

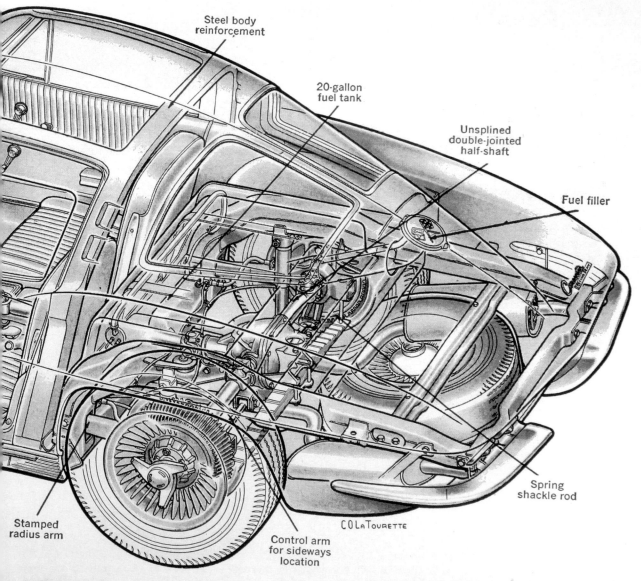

Steel body reinforcement

20-gallon fuel tank

Unsplined double-jointed half-shaft

Fuel filler

Spring shackle rod

Stamped radius arm

Control arm for sideways location

COLaTourette

CORVETTE CONTINUED

Engineering in the enviable position of rear-suspension pioneers in this country, and one might think that Duntov had long been known as an expert on suspension geometry. But before he joined Chevrolet, he was best known for his special camshafts and the Ardun overhead-valve conversions for flat-head Ford and Mercury V-8s. For several years he was the associate of Sydney H. Allard, who manufactured the Allard sports car in London, and Duntov even partnered Sydney Allard in racing, notably at Le Mans. He already had considerable racing experience with Porsches in Europe, which may have had something to do with his interest in rear-engined cars.

Duntov remains non-committal about his early past and future racing plans, both for himself and for the new Corvettes. As pointed out in last month's C/D, only the sport coupé will be available with heavy-duty (i.e., racing) options. We hope that Chevrolet has plans to race the car officially, a thought which brings only a smile to Duntov's lips, but apparently no decision has been made yet.

Perhaps optimism on this point is more realistic than generally realized. Chevrolet's general manager, Semon E. (Bunky) Knudsen, came to this job from Pontiac, where he was responsible for bringing that make into the front rank of speedy sedans. With a genuine sports car on his hands, and an attitude several degrees off perfect alignment with the AMA resolution, he may find the means of letting Duntov take up where he left off in 1957. Surely this would be the logical thing, for nobody at Chevrolet Engineering, least of all Zora Arkus-Duntov, allows himself to forget that they have to have a still better Corvette ten years from now. **C/D**

The experimental **CERV**-1 helped develop the independent rear suspension that was adapted to the 1963 Corvette Sting Ray, with alterations caused only by styling and space requirements.

With a 327-cubic-inch **V-8** and disc brakes on all four wheels, the first Sting Ray is a better car today than when it was raced.

There's a groove in every curve...
for Corvettes!

Well, that's what it *feels* like! And that feeling—the solid road-gripping security, the superb sense of control and command—is something that only the genuine *sports car* can give you.

What's the feeling worth? Very little, if you're not much interested in driving for its own sake. But if you are, nothing man has ever built can produce the same dazzling surge of delight!

Seriously, here's a test you should try if you want to know just how much pure pleasure you can pack into motoring: Borrow a Corvette, pick a stretch of wickedly curving road that you really respect—and bore into it. Surprise! What happened to the bends that used to set the tail wagging, the car drifting out toward the

center line, the body tilting? Sure, they're the same curves—but this is the way a car ought to go round them. Flat, locked in its own lane, riding the radius as though in an invisible groove!

What *kind* of a Corvette should you choose for this test? Any one, from the competition version with 283-h.p. fuel injection V8* and four-speed gearbox* to the butter-smooth Powerglide* town car. There are all sorts of engine, transmission and luxury equipment options. But we make only one kind of chassis—the honest-to-Pete sports car kind, with road-holding no other car in America can match! Try it—and see what it feels like to find a groove in every curve! . . . *Chevrolet Division of General Motors, Detroit 2, Mich.* *Optional at extra cost.

CORVETTE

by Chevrolet

Waiting lists of great length and duration for the Corvette Sting Ray at all Chevrolet dealers' are the best proof of the public's acceptance of the new model. We hailed the car's technical advances with great enthusiasm (*Oct. C/D*) after our brief test drives last fall.

Now it's time for an exhaustive report on America's leading grand touring car (which many drivers think of only as a sports car). We chose the 300-bhp version of the coupé, because it seems to enjoy some market preference over models equipped with the 250-, 340-, or fuel-injection 360-bhp engines.

However, the key to the personality of the Corvette Sting Ray lies neither in the power available nor in the revised styling, but in the chassis. Up to now the Corvette has been struggling to rise above a large number of stock components, notably in the suspension, where their presence created all kinds of problems that re-

quired extensive modifications for any competition use beyond normal road rallies. The new all-independent suspension has completely transformed the Corvette in terms of traction and cornering power, but it still has some faults. The standard setup on the test car seemed a bit more suitable for race tracks than for fast back-road motoring. A rigid front anti-roll bar in combination with a relatively stiff transverse leaf spring in the rear reduces the resilience and independence of the suspension of each wheel with the result that even on mildly rough surfaces the car does not feel perfectly stable. On bumpy turns it's at its worst, veering freely from one course to another, making high-frequency corrections s.o.p., but on a smooth surface it comes incredibly close to perfection. Cornering stability under conditions permitting minimal wheel deflections is remarkable, and an initial feeling of pleasant surprise

At long last America has a formidable weapon to challenge

CAR and DRIVER ROAD RESEARCH REPORT:

Corvette Sting Ray

rises to sheer astonishment when one discovers that the car can be taken off the predetermined line with ease and still complete the turn in perfect balance.

There is some understeer but the car has such a tremendous power surplus, even with the next-to-bottom engine option, that the tail can be slung out almost any old time, and after a while throttle steering seems the natural way of aiding the car around a curve. This is so easy to do that a newcomer to the car can master it in half an hour of fast driving.

Given surface roughness, the rear end becomes skittish. We experienced this with a full tank as well as one almost empty, indicating that normal loads don't appreciably affect its behavior in this respect.

One of our test cars had the new Saginaw power steering, three turns lock to lock with enough road feel to satisfy the most critical tester and observer, while eliminating all difficulties of parking and maneuvering in tight spaces. We also tested a car with manual steering, and found it so light in comparison with previous Corvettes that there can be no conceivable need for power assistance. While the power system is every bit as good as those used by Rover and Mercedes-Benz in terms of feedback and road feel, it seems strange that Chevrolet should get around to introducing it when there is no longer any need for it. The three-spoke wheel is steeply raked (15° 23') as on previous Corvettes, and its relatively thin rim offers a good grip. The entire semi-circle between nine and three o'clock is free of spoke attachments, providing a clean hold for any but the most eccentric drivers. The steering column has a three-inch adjustment for length but our test drivers all kept the wheel in its foremost (bottom) position while making the most of seat-adjustment possibilities. There

Europe's fastest grand touring cars on their home ground

CORVETTE STING RAY CONTINUED

are four inches of fore-and-aft travel but backrest angle is variable only by setting screws at its floor abutments. In addition, there are three seat-height positions with a total span of 1.24 inches.

The result is a range of adjustment adequate to let our test drivers (ranging in height from five-seven to six-four) find a nearly ideal seating position. Maximum effective leg room (to the accelerator) is 43.7 inches and the maximum vertical height from the seat to the headlining is 33 inches. In view of the over-all height of only 49.8 inches, this is a good example of the care that has gone into designing the living quarters of the new Corvette Sting Ray.

As the engine and drive train are offset one inch to the right to provide wider leg room for the driver, he sits facing exactly in the direction he is going, with the pedals straight in front of him. The accelerator is nicely angled for normally disposed feet, but the clutch pedal has a rather excessive travel. With standard adjustment, you cannot release it without taking your heel off the floor, causing a bit of annoyance in traffic.

Instead of a fly-off handbrake, the Corvette has a T-handle under the instrument panel labeled "Parking Brake"—one of the few features of the new model which reminds you of its relationship with Chevrolet's mass-produced sedans.

Compared with previous Corvettes, the Sting Ray is improved in almost every imaginable respect: performance, handling, ride comfort, habitability and trunk space. The trunk is only accessible from inside the car, however, since the tail is full of fuel tank and spare wheel, but the storage space behind the seats is even larger than outside dimensions indicate. A third person, sitting sideways, may come along for short rides, but will soon feel cramped from lack of headroom. An occasional extra passenger will actually be better off sitting on the console between the seats and sharing legroom with the shotgun rider.

Having driven the Corvette Sport Coupé in all kinds of weather conditions, we found the heater and defroster units eminently satisfactory. The heater fan has

three speeds, and air entry is variable by a push-pull control. Warm-up is not extremely rapid but seems to be faster than average. The body proved absolutely draft-proof and water-tight.

We liked the ball-shaped interior door handles but were not convinced of the advantages of the wheel-type door lock buttons. A minor complaint is the location of the window winders, as you cannot set your knee against the door panel for bracing on a sharp turn without coming in contact with the window handle.

Brakes have long been a sore point with Corvettes, and further advance has now been made without taking the full step of going to disc brakes (which the car really deserves). The Delco-Moraine power brakes have 11-inch steel drums cast into the wheel rims, with 58.8% of the braking force being directed to the front wheels. Sintered iron brake linings are optional and will certainly be found necessary for anyone planning to race, as fade is easily provoked with the standard linings, although the cooling-off period required to restore full efficiency is very short.

Chevrolet is prepared for a fair-sized demand for special performance parts, but has restricted their application to the structurally stronger Sport Coupé. The sintered-iron heavy-duty brake system also includes vented backing plates and air scoops and a dual-circuit master cylinder. There is a heavy-duty anti-roll bar, heavy-duty front and rear shock absorbers, aluminum wheels with knock-off hubs, and a 36-gallon fuel tank. The brake mechanism, in contrast to that fitted as standard, automatically adjusts the brakes when applied during *forward* motion. To be ordered, this special performance kit (RPO ZO6) also requires the 360-bhp engine, the four-speed Warner T-10 gearbox and a Positraction limited-slip differential.

Race preparation of the 327-cubic-inch Corvette engine has been thoroughly treated by Bill Thomas in an article for the *Corvette News* (Volume 5 No. 3), a GM publication invaluable to both the active Corvette competitor and his "civilian" counterpart. For information, readers are advised to write to *Corvette News,* 205 GM Building, Detroit 2, Michigan.

For all kinds of non-competitive driving, the 300-

Body was wind-tunnel tested but many

Luggage space is surprisingly roomy but central window partition ruins rear view.

A ventilated fuel filler cap is reached through lid. Gear positions are labeled.

bhp version gives more than ample performance for anyone, with our average standing-quarter-mile time at 14.4 seconds. This was achieved with the "street" gearbox and an axle ratio which limits top speed to about 118 mph, a combination which results in extreme top-gear flexibility as well. Top-gear starts from standstill to limit wheelspin present no problem with regard to stalling, but detonations were inevitable.

Fiberglass bodies usually have peculiar noises all their own but the Corvette was remarkably quiet, no doubt due to the steel reinforcement surrounding the entire passenger compartment. The car is also notable for low wind noise and high directional stability. Engine noise is largely dependent on the throttle opening —it will respond with a roar to a wiggle of the toe if you're wearing light shoes, and this holds true within an extremely broad speed range. Top-gear acceleration from 50 to 80 is impressive indeed, both in sound and abdominal effects.

In this connection, the gear lever has a set of speeds at which it vibrates and generates a high-pitched rattle (this is in the lever itself and not in the reverse catch), and there are intermittent peculiar noises from the clock, probably when it rewinds itself.

The now-familiar Warner T-10 gearbox has faultless synchromesh and when fully broken in can be as light as cutting butter. One interesting aspect of its operation is the fact that the owner's handbook specifies double-clutching for down-shifts.

We are in complete agreement with this recommendation, over which there has been some controversy. Some people feel that double-clutching will wear out the synchromesh. This can be true only if on downshifts the engine is accelerated so much that the synchromesh has to work harder than it would with a single-clutch change, a situation which does not seem to occur very often.

While we agree that the Buick Riviera, for example, is the kind of car where automatic transmission has a function, we cannot see its place in the Corvette and our testing was done exclusively on a pair of manual-shift cars, one with power steering and one without, neither with Positraction limited-slip differential, which

object to superfluous decoration by emblems and dummy vents.

perhaps should be standard equipment on this car.

As the majority of new Corvettes are built with four-speed transmissions, it is hard to understand why the three-speed remains listed as standard equipment. We can see no reason for even continuing to offer it, and recommend that both the Powerglide and the three-speed manual gearbox be dropped. This would let Chevrolet standardize the wide-ratio four-speed transmission throughout and make the close-ratio version optional for the 340- and 360-bhp models.

Our testers preferred the car with the fewest automatic "aids," and probably most of our readers will, too. That keen drivers prefer manual controls is not baffling at all—except possibly to advanced research personnel who forget that nowhere else can they get an effective 180-pound corrective computer which can be produced at low cost by unskilled labor.

Vastly more practical than any previous Corvette, the Sting Ray Sport Coupé appeals to a new segment of buyers who would not be interested in a convertible, and production schedules at the Saint Louis assembly plant have been doubled from the 1962 model's. As an American car it is unique, and it stands out from its European counterparts as having in no way copied them but arrived at the same goal along a different route. Zora Arkus-Duntov summed it up this way: "For the first time I now have a Corvette I can be proud to drive in Europe." We understand his feelings and are happy to agree that the Sting Ray is a fine showpiece for the American auto industry, especially since it is produced at a substantially lower price than any foreign sports or GT car of comparable performance. **C/D**

Directional and parking lights are part of bumper design but the retractable headlamps are concealed for daytime driving.

The Corvette is perhaps best looking from behind, and this is a view that drivers of other cars will soon become used to.

CONTINUED 39

Road Research Report
Chevrolet Corvette Sting Ray Sport Coupe

Manufacturer: Chevrolet Motor Division
General Motors Corporation
Detroit 2, Michigan

Number of U.S. dealers: 7,000 (approximately)
Planned annual production: 16,000

PRICES
Basic price $4,252

OPERATING SCHEDULE
Fuel recommended .... Premium (99-101 Octane)
Mileage .... 10-18 mpg
Range on 20-gallon tank .... 200-360 miles
Oil recommended   Single grade   Multi-grade
32° F and over .... SAE 20 or 20W   SAE 10W-30
0° F .... SAE 10W   SAE 10W-30
below 0° F .... SAE 5W   SAE 5W-20
Crankcase capacity .... 5 quarts
Change at intervals of .... 6,000 miles
Number of grease fittings .... 10 (9 with manual steering)
Most frequent maintenance .... Lubrication at every 6,000 miles

ENGINE:
Displacement .... 327 cu in, 5,370 cc
Dimensions .... 8 cyl, 4.00-in bore, 3.25-in stroke
Valve gear: ...... Pushrod-operated overhead valves (hydraulic lifters)
Compression ratio .... 10.5 to one
Power (SAE) .... 300 bhp @ 5,000 rpm
Torque .... 360 lb-ft @ 3,200 rpm
Usable range of engine speeds .... 600-5,500 rpm
Carburetion .... Single four-throat Carter WCFB carburetor

CHASSIS:
Wheelbase .... 98 in
Track .... F 56.3 in, R 57.0 in
Length .... 175.3 in
Ground clearance .... 7.5 in
Suspension: F: Ind., coil springs and wishbones, anti-roll bar
         R: Ind., lower wishbones and unsplined half-shafts acting as
         locating members, radius arms and transverse leaf spring
Steering .... Saginaw recirculating ball with power assistance
Turns, lock to lock 3
Turning circle diameter between curbs .... 36 ft
Tire size .... 6.70 x 15
Pressures recommended .... F 24, R 24 psi
Brakes .... Delco-Moraine 11-in drums front and rear, 328 sq in swept area
Curb weight (full tank) .... 3,180 lbs
Percentage on the driving wheels 53

DRIVE TRAIN:

Gear	Synchro	Ratio	Step	Over-all	1,000 rpm
Clutch		Borg & Beck 10-in single dry plate			
Rev	No	2.61	—	8.78	−9.0
1st	Yes	2.54	34%	8.52	9.3
2nd	Yes	1.89	25%	6.36	12.4
3rd	Yes	1.51	51%	5.08	15.6
4th	Yes	1.00	—	3.36	23.5
Final drive ratio					3.36 to one

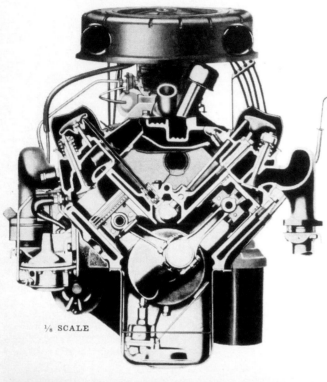

⅛ SCALE

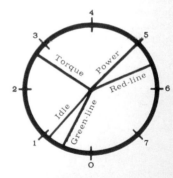

Steering Behavior
Wheel position to
maintain 400-foot circle
at speeds indicated.

Goodyear
6.70 x 15
F 24 psi
R 24 psi

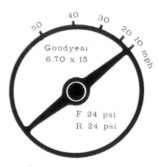

Engine Flexibility
RPM in thousands

Torque   Power
Idle   Red-line
Green-line

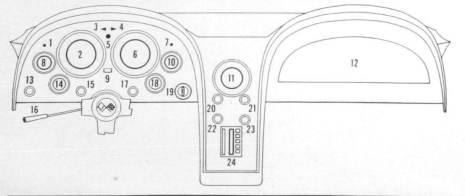

(1) Turn signal warning light (left); (2) Speedometer and odometer; (3) Warning light for headlights on in closed position; (4) Parking brake warning light; (5) High beam warning light; (6) Tachometer; (7) Turn signal warning light (right); (8) Water temperature gauge; (9) Trip odometer; (10) Oil pressure gauge; (11) Clock; (12) Glove box; (13) Light switch; (14) Ammeter; (15) Windshield wiper and washer; (16) Turn signal lever; (17) Cigarette lighter; (18) Fuel gauge; (19) Ignition key and starter; (20) Heater fan and fresh air control; (21) Defroster control; (22) Radio volume and tone control; (23) Radio tuning selector; (24) Radio dial.

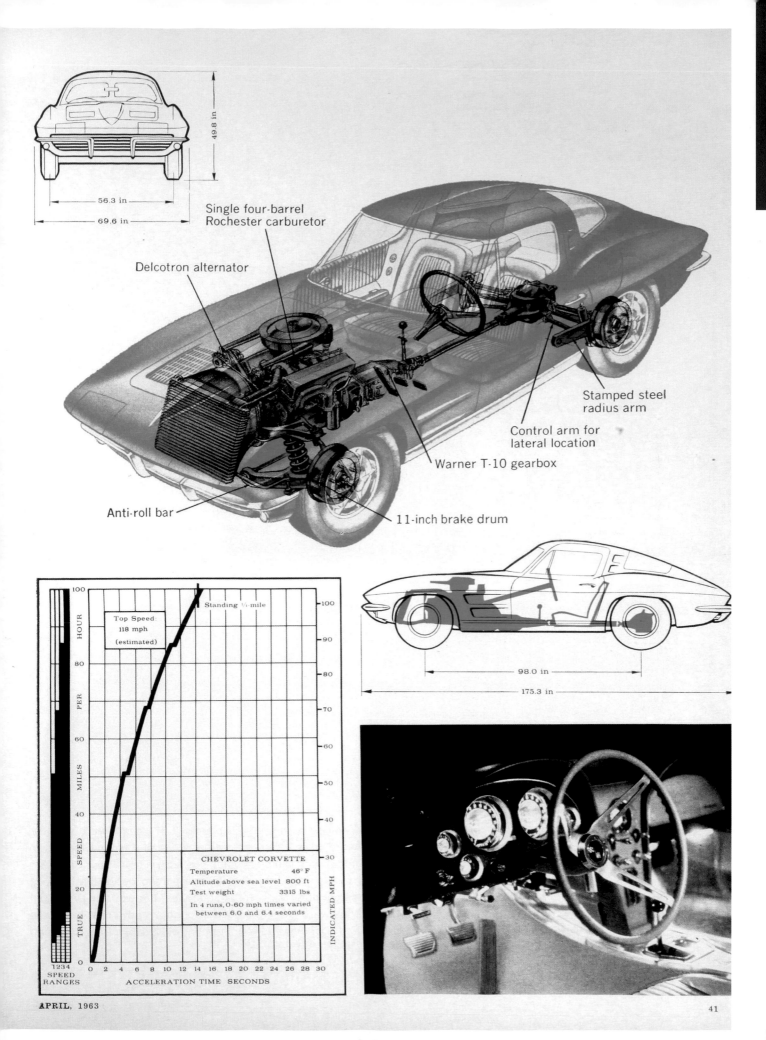

56.3 in

69.6 in

49.8 in

Single four-barrel
Rochester carburetor

Delcotron alternator

Stamped steel
radius arm

Control arm for
lateral location

Warner T-10 gearbox

Anti-roll bar

11-inch brake drum

98.0 in

175.3 in

CHEVROLET CORVETTE

Temperature   46° F
Altitude above sea level 800 ft
Test weight   3315 lbs

In 4 runs, 0-60 mph times varied
between 6.0 and 6.4 seconds

Top Speed:
118 mph
(estimated)

Standing ¼-mile

HOUR   PER   MILES   SPEED   TRUE

1234
SPEED
RANGES

ACCELERATION TIME SECONDS

INDICATED MPH

S teering gets plenty quick at 140 mph. And the suspension, which felt like flint on Sunset Strip, is supple, almost loose. In this high-velocity never-neverland all your senses need reorientation: A road that looks mirror flat pitches you violently up and down; the air makes tortured noises you hear right through the glass as it scrapes over the top of the windshield; an unseen force slowly twists and tortures the outside mirror until it surrenders and ends up pointing skyward.

Keeping the car, and yourself, on the straight and narrow is so much a hairtrigger operation that it takes your logical conscience about three miles to break through your concentration—you haven't got time to carry on a mental debate about the morality of what you are doing. But when that logical, practical conscience does break through, it is not amused. Bad enough to spend a day driving to Nevada, but to tempt the worst kind of destruction by running a 454 Corvette right up to the redline in top gear and hold it there is damn near unAmerican. There is no defense. No rational excuse for driving along at *double* the posted speed limits in any other state.

Rationale be damned; plead "temporary enthusiasm" and get it over with. And get back to the beauty of it. Because that's

The Corvette Test

C/D AND ZORA ARKUS-DUNTOV COMPARE THE FULL RANGE OF CORVETTES 270-HP L48 · 330-HP LT1 365-HP LS5 · 425-HP LS6

what happens. It happens to anybody who spends a few days with Zora Arkus-Duntov testing Corvettes of every engine description that Chevrolet makes in 1971: running them on the drag strip, around the skid pad and through a makeshift road course. And all the time talking to Duntov about it, about what he did to the suspension and the tires and the aerodynamics so that the Corvette is the only car built in

PHOTOGRAPHY: HUMPHREY SUTTON

America that can run 140 mph no sweat and the driver doesn't have to worry about becoming history.

Later, when the driving is finished for the day, there is dinner and maybe a few drinks and more talk—talk about what it was like back when the Delahayes and the Talbots were trying to knock off the Mercedes and Auto Union juggernauts on the Grand Prix circuit; about how Duntov got the idea for the "Ardun" cylinderhead conversion while driving his flat-head Ford wide open across France one day before the war; about what it was like to work with Sydney Allard and drive an Allard at Le Mans and lose, then to switch to

Porsche and win the class the next two years in a row.

But whether it is between courses at dinner or while the condensation was running down a Martini glass, Corvettes are never far below the surface. Little by little glimpses of automotive history would come out—things that put today, and the 1971 Corvette, into perspective: That he had worked with a brilliant engineer named John Dolza on the Rochester fuel-injection and the system is fundamentally sound today except that cubic inches are a cheaper way to horsepower; that the "Duntov" cam was an emergency horsepower device he developed when Chevrolet wanted to crack 150 mph on Daytona Beach in 1956; the contempt Duntov feels for the body shape of the 1963-1967 Sting Ray because it had "just enough lift to be a bad airplane."

There are discussions of current technology and sketches on napkins; penciled-in arrows show that air doesn't enter the radiator of the current Corvette through the grille—it is blocked off by the license plates and the head light shields—instead air is shoveled up by a spoiler below and behind the grille and enters the bodywork through two slots you can't even see unless you lie down in front of the car.

There is an answer for every question and a reason for every one of the Corvette's characteristics. Duntov will talk of the battles and compromises that have been thrashed out between him and the stylists, product planners, and memo writers but he is adamant about one feature—throughout production he has stood firmly against those who would have reduced the Corvette's stability at high speed.

That is why tires are designed specifical-

WHO BUYS A CORVETTE

Sex: 93% are male
Marital status: 56% are single
Median age: 26.6 years
Education: 52% have graduated from college
　　　　　85% have attended college
　　　　　20% have attended graduate school
Job: 35% are professional or managerial
　　(largest category)
　　12% are in the military
Family size: 2.4 in household
Income: $15,500 average household income

WHAT THEY BOUGHT IN 1970

Coupes	62.0%
Convertibles	38.0%
Automatic transmission	29.5%
4-Speed transmission	70.5%

Engines:

300-bhp 350 (std)	38.4%
350-bhp 350 (L46)	28.4%
370-bhp 350 (LT1)	7.4%
390-bhp 454 (LS5)	25.8%
Radio	98.1%
Power steering	68.8%
Power brakes	51.9%
Power windows	27.8%
Stripe or white letter tires	84.2%
Air conditioning	38.5%
Wheel covers	20.0%
Movable steering column	33.5%
Rear window defroster	7.2%
Speed warning device	10.4%
Transistor ignition	16.6%

ly for the Corvette—N44 nylon cord—good for sustained 140 mph driving and they are used on *no* other American car. Duntov knows it is against the law to travel at that speed in every state but one and he doesn't care. If any Corvette driver, for whatever reason, should have occasion to drive at 140 mph the capability to do so safely should be built into the car. It's built into the suspension; the Corvette has more suspension travel than any other car manufactured in this country. If Duntov and the engineers desired, this travel would allow them to make a soft ride—softer than any of the performance cars—but then the Corvette would be likely to bottom out at high speed and it would be unstable. So the ride stays hard even if there is excessive travel by Detroit standards; that's the price you pay for 140-mph capability.

The same design priority comes out again and again in discussions of brakes, steering, aerodynamics—the concern for the Corvette driver who may some day run his pinched-waist two-seater up to the redline *and hold it there.* Traditionally, top

31

speed is something that only European car builders worry about. But when Duntov speaks, and you break your concentration on what he is saying long enough to notice *how* he says it, you know that he is closer to them than us. Although born in Belgium, he is a Russian, and all of the years after he left Russia—studying engineering in Germany, occupying his spare time with racing motorcycles and cars; the years in Belgium and France working on race cars and the highest output engines of the day (often supercharged)—have had as profound an effect on his automotive philosophy as on his accent. And his accent is a hardened alloy of old world structures and formations that 30 years in the United States seem not to have scratched.

So you focus on the way he says his words, a way that is his alone, and you feel the intensity of his commitment to the Corvette and to engineering it to a level of performance surpassing all of the volume production cars in the world. Then, almost without noticing the transition, you find yourself in Nevada with the tachometer

just a needle-width away from the red zone. The speedometer reads over 140 mph and you know that everything is all right, if it can ever be all right in any car, at that speed, because Zora Arkus-Duntov would settle for nothing less.

Obviously this is no ordinary road test. But then how could it be when it's about a man so rare and complex as Duntov and about cars so Detroit-yet-European as the Corvette. At this point it would be the worst kind of irresponsible journalism to say that Duntov is personally responsible for every nut, bolt and forging in the Corvette—dozens of Chevrolet engineers work on it. Still, over the years, it has been *his*

vision of what a high-performance sports car should be that has transformed the descendants of the bulbous, indifferent 1953 Corvette into a two-place touring machine that can be successfully raced in the international GT category. So when you can have him—Chevrolet Chief Engineer-Corvette—present at the test to drive and explain why the 1971 Corvette behaves the way it does, the results have to be more meaningful.

The project was simple at the start. Every year for the last five years *C/D* readers have voted the Corvette as Best All-Around Car in the world, bar none. Any car with that strong a rating deserves an in-depth review. That means all of the Corvettes, one with each engine. And a little patience, for unless you plan months in advance, having the whole cast show up in one place on one day is impossible. We settled for two on one day and three a few weeks later—the LT1 being in the line-up twice—and were fortunate in having Duntov present for both sessions.

The test cars were all coupes as is the majority (62%) of the production run. While having at least one convertible in the test would have allowed an examination of that model, it would have also added an undesirable variable. The different sound qualities of the two body styles and the different car weights would have certainly clouded the clear picture we now have of the various engines.

This is not to say that to have a valid test all participating cars should be equipped alike except for the engine. On the contrary, the Corvette has great latitude—it can be optioned as a luxury tourer or as a high-performance sports car—but

(text continued on page 90)

32

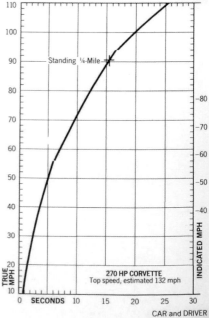

270hp L48

List Price as tested: $6538.80

Options on test car: Power steering, $115.90; power brakes, $47.40; power windows, $85.35; AM/FM radio, $178.00; air conditioning, $464.50; tilt-telescope steering wheel, $84.30; white stripe tires, $30.35

ENGINE

Bore x stroke	4.00 x 3.48 in
Displacement	350 cu in
Compression ratio	8.5 to one
Carburetion	1 x 4-bbl Rochester
Power (SAE)	270 bhp @ 4800 rpm
Torque (SAE)	360 lb-ft @ 3200 rpm
Max recommended engine speed	5500 rpm

DRIVE TRAIN

Transmission			3-speed automatic
Max. torque converter			2.1
Final drive ratio			3.08 to one
Gear	Ratio	Mph/1000 rpm	Max test speed
I	2.48	10.2	56 mph (5500 rpm)
II	1.48	17.0	94 mph (5500 rpm)
III	1.00	25.2	113 mph (4500 rpm)

DIMENSIONS AND CAPACITIES

Wheelbase	98.0 in
Track	F: 58.7 in, R: 59.4 in
Length	182.5 in
Width	69.0 in
Height	47.8 in
Curb weight	3460 lbs
Weight distribution, F/R	50.1/49.9%
Fuel capacity	18.0 gal
Oil capacity	4.0 qts
Water capacity	15.0 qts

SUSPENSION

F: Ind., unequal length control arms, coil springs, anti-sway bar
R: Ind., single trailing arm positioned laterally by a single strut and a fixed-length half shaft, transverse leaf spring

STEERING

Type	Recirculating ball, linkage booster
Turns lock-to-lock	3.4

WHEELS AND TIRES

Wheel size	15 x 8.0
Tire make and size	Firestone F70-15

PERFORMANCE

Zero to	seconds
40 mph	3.6
60 mph	7.1
80 mph	12.3
100 mph	19.8
Standing 1/4-mile	15.55 sec @ 90.36 mph
Top speed (estimated)	132 mph
80-0 mph	238 ft (0.90 G)
Fuel mileage	12.0-15.0 mpg on regular fuel

270 HP CORVETTE
Top speed, estimated 132 mph

Standing ¼-Mile

TRUE MPH

INDICATED MPH

SECONDS

330hp LT1

List Price as tested: $6742.60

Options on test car: 330-hp 350 engine, $483,45; power steering, $115.90; power brakes, $47.40; power windows, $85.35; AM/FM stereo radio, $283.35; tilt-telescope steering wheel, $84.30; wheel covers, $63.20; white-letter tires, $43.65

ENGINE

Bore x stroke	4.00 x 3.48 in
Displacement	350 cu in
Compression ratio	9.0 to one
Carburetion	1 x 4-bbl Holley
Power (SAE)	330 bhp @ 5600 rpm
Torque (SAE)	360 lb-ft @ 4000 rpm
Max recommended engine speed	6500 rpm

DRIVE TRAIN

Transmission .... 4-speed, all-synchro
Final drive ratio .... 3.70 to one

Gear	Ratio	Mph/1000rpm	Max. test speed
I	2.20	9.6	62 mph (6500 rpm)
II	1.64	12.8	83 mph (6500 rpm)
III	1.27	16.5	107 mph (6500 rpm)
IV	1.00	21.1	129 mph (6100 rpm)

DIMENSIONS AND CAPACITIES

Wheelbase	98.0 in
Track	F: 58.7 in, R: 59.4 in
Length	182.5 in
Width	69.0 in
Height	47.8 in
Curb weight	3370 lbs
Weight distribution, F/R	49.2/50.8%
Fuel capacity	18.0 gal
Oil Capacity	5.0 qts
Water capacity	18.0 qts

SUSPENSION

F: Ind., unequal length control arms, coil springs, anti-sway bar
R: Ind., single trailing arm positioned laterally by a single strut and a fixed-length half shaft, transverse leaf spring

STEERING

Type	Recirculating ball, linkage booster
Turns lock-to-lock	3.4

WHEELS AND TIRES

Wheel size	15 x 8.0 in
Tire make and size	Firestone F70-15

PERFORMANCE

Zero to	seconds
40 mph	3.4
60 mph	6.0
80 mph	9.7
100 mph	14.5

Standing 1/4-mile .... 14.57 sec @ 100.55 mph
Top speed (at redline) .... 137 mph
80-0 mph .... 237 ft (0.90 G)
Fuel mileage .... 11.0-16.0 mpg on premium fuel

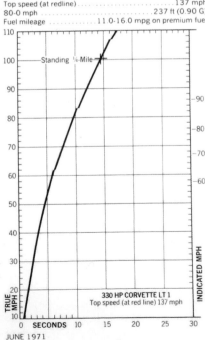

330 HP CORVETTE LT 1
Top speed (at red line) 137 mph

365hp LS5

List Price as tested: $7255.85

Options on test car: 365-hp 454 engine, $294.90; automatic transmission, $100.35; power steering, $115.90; power brakes, $47.40; power windows, $85.35; custom leather trim, $158.00; AM/FM stereo radio, $283.35; rear window defroster, $42.15; tilt-telescope steering wheel, $84.30; white-letter tires, $43.65; air conditioning, $464.50

ENGINE

Bore x stroke	4.25 x 4.00 in
Displacement	454 cu in
Compression ratio	8.5 to one
Carburetion	1 x 4-bbl Rochester
Power (SAE)	365 bhp @ 4800 rpm
Torque (SAE)	465 lb-ft @ 3200 rpm
Max recommended engine speed	5600 rpm

DRIVE TRAIN

Transmission .... 3-speed, automatic
Max torque converter .... 2.1 to one
Final drive ratio .... 3.08 to one

Gear	Ratio	Mph/1000rpm	Max. test speed
I	2.48	10.2	57 mph (5600 rpm)
II	1.48	17.0	95 mph (5600 rpm)
III	1.00	25.2	141 mph (5600 rpm)

DIMENSIONS AND CAPACITIES

Wheelbase	98.0 in
Track	F: 58.7 in, 59.4 in
Length	182.5 in
Width	69.0 in
Height	47.8 in
Curb weight	3675 lbs
Weight distribution, F/R	51.6/48.4%
Fuel capacity	18.0 gal
Oil capacity	5.0 qts
Water capacity	22.0 qts

SUSPENSION

F: Ind., unequal length control arms, coil springs, anti-sway bar
R: Ind., single trailing arm positioned laterally by a single strut and a fixed-length half shaft, transverse leaf spring, anti-sway bar

STEERING

Type	Recirculating ball, linkage booster
Turns lock-to-lock	3.4

WHEELS AND TIRES

Wheel size	15 x 8.0 in
Tire make and size	Goodyear F70-15

PERFORMANCE

Zero to	seconds
40 mph	3.0
60 mph	5.7
80 mph	9.3
100 mph	14.1

Standing 1/4-mile .... 14.20 sec @ 100.33 mph
Top speed (2-way avg.) .... 141 mph
80-0 mph .... 260 ft (0.82 G)
Fuel mileage .... 8.0-11.0 mpg on regular fuel

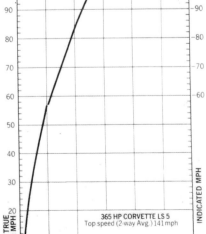

365 HP CORVETTE LS 5
Top speed (2-way Avg) 141 mph

425hp LS6

List Price as tested: $7619.35

Options on test car: 425-hp 454 engine, $1220.70; M22 4-speed transmission, $100.35; power brakes, $47.40; power steering, $115.90; power windows, $85.35; rear window defroster, $42.15; tilt-telescope steering wheel, $84.30; white-letter tires, $43.65; custom wheel covers, $63.20; AM/FM stereo radio, $283.35

ENGINE

Bore x stroke	4.25 x 4.00 in
Displacement	454 cu in
Compression ratio	9.0 to one
Carburetion	1 x 4-bbl Holley
Power (SAE)	425 bhp @ 5600 rpm
Torque (SAE)	475 lb-ft @ 4000
Max recommended engine speed	6500 rpm

DRIVE TRAIN

Transmission .... 4-speed, all-synchro
Final drive ratio .... 3.36 to one

Gear	Ratio	Mph/1000rpm	Max. test speed
I	2.20	10.5	68 mph (6500 rpm)
II	1.64	14.2	92 mph (6500 rpm)
III	1.27	18.2	118 mph (6500 rpm)
IV	1.00	23.2	137 mph (6500 rpm)

DIMENSIONS AND CAPACITIES

Wheelbase	98.0 in
Track	F: 58.7 in, R: 59.4 in
Length	182.5 in
Width	69.0 in
Height	47.8 in
Curb weight	3478 lbs
Weight distribution, F/R	50.1/49.9%
Fuel capacity	18.0 gal
Oil capacity	5/0 qts
Water capacity	20.0 qts

SUSPENSION

F: Ind., unequal length control arms, coil springs, anti-sway bar
R: Ind., single trailing arm positioned laterally by a single strut and a fixed-length half shaft, transverse leaf spring, anti-sway bar

STEERING

Type	Recirculating ball, linkage booster
Turns lock-to-lock	3.4

WHEELS AND TIRES

Wheel size	15 x 8.0 in
Tire make and size	Goodyear F70-15

PERFORMANCE

Zero to	seconds
40 mph	3.0
60 mph	5.3
80 mph	8.5
100 mph	12.7

Standing 1/4-mile .... 13.80 sec @ 104.65 mph
Top speed (at redline) .... 152 mph
80-0 mph .... 251 ft (0.85 G)
Fuel mileage .... 9.0-14.0 mpg on premium fuel

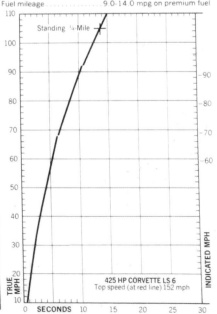

425 HP CORVETTE LS 6
Top speed (at red line) 152 mph

CORVETTES

(Continued from page 32)

the difference should hinge on the choice of engine. So we've divided the test cars into those two categories. Both touring cars have the low-compression, hydraulic-lifter engines and the relaxed nature of the powerplants is complemented by automatic transmissions and air conditioners. The performance models are equally distinct in their roles; higher-compression, mechanical lifter engines with close-ratio 4-speed transmissions, and to keep the weight down, no air conditioning. All of the cars have Chevrolet's "standard" axle ratio for the engine/transmission combination.

Clearly, the 350 cu.in. 270-hp Corvette engine does not fall in the performance category. It is the lowest output 4-bbl. V-8 Chevrolet builds (available as an option in every model except the Vega) and it specializes in painless performance. It is quiet and completely without vice. Those who want to be comfortable and avoid the mechanical hassle but still go fast should opt for the LS5, the 365-hp 454. It's every bit as relaxed as the base engine but an ox for strength, able to turn an air conditioner compressor and quick quarter miles at the same time. Just don't forget the gas money.

But those powerplants are of little interest to the Corvette purist, the man who remembers the soul and vitality of the high-winding fuel-injected 283 when it was the only street engine in the country that put out one horsepower per cubic inch. Today's equivalent is the LT1—a solid-lifter 350 rated at 330-hp. The compression ratio has been dropped to 9.0-to-one this year, a giant step down from the 11.25 that some of the small-block Corvettes have had in the past, but it hasn't lost the vibrant, high-strung personality that made it famous. It's eager and it talks to you. Today it is probably even better known as the Z28, which is what it is called when ordered in the Camaro. Corvette engineers originated the idea so Duntov winces when you say the two engines are the same, but they are. Somehow, though, it seems less subdued in the Corvette, perhaps because of the fiber glass body which acts as less of a barrier to sound than the steel of the Camaro. In the LT1 you're always aware of the clatter from the solid lifters and the exhaust pipes radiate sound right up through the floor. It's a frustrated racer, a fact it nevers lets you forget.

If you want the fastest Corvette, however, there is no confusion. Order the LS6—the 425-hp 454. It's like the LT1 only bigger. The LS6 is available in other Chevrolets, certainly in the Chevelle, but not with exactly the same equipment that makes up

the Corvette package. It's a premium quality engine from the very core—double-shot-peened connecting rods, tuftrided crank, forged pistons—and you pay for it: $1220.70 as an option. But no corners have been cut. The price includes transistorized ignition, a double disc clutch (which not only has lower pedal effort and shorter travel but also enough torque capacity for long life even with a 3.08 axle ratio), and aluminum heads (which save 55 lbs.). It's Duntov's favorite engine and he's tortured because few customers can afford it.

"Maybe for street engine I make mistake—aluminum heads are expensive and that weight doesn't matter on the street." But he's not going to compromise the performance just to take money out. And he has harsh words for the "bean counters" who occasionally eliminate a worthwhile option or feature. The L46 for example. Until this year you could buy a 350 cu.in. 350-hp engine with a hydraulic camshaft that had very nearly the performance of the LT1 but was also compatible with air

---

Zora Arkus-Duntov's goal is to provide Corvette drivers with the equipment they need—as opposed to what they think *they need—in a high performance road car.*

---

conditioning. And you could buy it for about $150 compared to $483 for the LT1. "Redundant," decided the bean counters and axed it off the list. Duntov thinks otherwise.

As for the engines that have survived, they have clearly suffered, not from the bean counters but at the hands of the emission control engineers. Dropping the compression ratio has pruned about 5% off the horsepower curves of all the Corvette engines and it shows up on the drag strip. The LS6 is fast, make no mistake—13.8 seconds at 104.65 mph for the quarter—but the three 2-bbl. 435-hp 427 tested two years ago (September '69) turned 106.8 mph. Axle ratios enter in here. While the 427 had a 3.70, the LS6 was hobbled with a 3.36 which not only means that you just hit third gear before the speed traps but makes getting a clean start more difficult.

The LS6 will definitely produce better times with a higher numerical axle ratio. And with a freer exhaust system. According to Duntov, 50 horsepower is lost in the

mufflers. That, however, is life. You have to have mufflers on the street. California laws say they have to be quiet ones and the LS6's are—stifled even. The pulses are still distinct—when each cylinder is pumping out over 50 horsepower they couldn't be otherwise—but they're muted. Giants in padded cells. (Chevrolet used to offer a chambered-pipe outside exhaust system that cost about 10 fewer horsepower than the mufflers but that's too loud now. . . .)

As you would expect, the personalities of the LS5 and the LT1 are worlds apart. In performance however, they are neck and neck. With the 454 automatic, just stand on it and go. Even though it is 305 lbs. heavier than the LT1, it reaches the end of the quarter about 0.3 seconds sooner. Like the LS6, the LT1 is very difficult to launch properly—the close-ratio gear box is not really suitable for standing start acceleration—so that even though the smaller engine Corvette is traveling faster at the end, it takes longer to get there. Naturally, the 270-hp model takes the longest of all to get there—15.55 seconds at 90.36 mph—and with its power-robbing options, it should be the slowest possible Corvette.

All of the Corvettes would be quicker if a cold air induction system were available. The discontinued L88 had one—a backwards facing hood scoop—but it also let a lot of engine noise seep out which California didn't like—and it was in conflict with the emission control hardware—so it was killed. (Duntov wouldn't admit to any plans to revive it.) Cold air to the carburetor is particularly helpful in a Corvette because it has the least underhood area of any 8-cylinder Chevrolet—which means it suffers the most from high underhood temperatures. You can see it from the drag strip results. Each succeeding run is slower than the previous one until a final equilibrium is reached, usually 1-2 mph slower than the first run following a cool-off period. The high engine compartment temperatures are also transferred into the cockpit. Considerable effort has been made to ventilate the underhood area more effectively, the front fender vents help, but not enough to make the passenger compartment comfortable in hot weather. So unless you are intent on straight-line performance, we recommend air conditioning.

Two different close-ratio 4-speeds are available on the Corvette, the normal one which Duntov says is plenty good enough for any kind of street use, and the M22, known as the "rock crusher" to those who can't remember M22. The difference be-

(Continued on page 92)

CORVETTES

(Continued from page 90)

tween the two is the gears—a little straighter cut on the teeth in the rock crusher—and a great deal of noise. Both of the boxes shift alike because the synchronizers are the same. And they shift very well because of the Corvette's excellent shift linkage. Unlike other Detroit 4-speeds, the Corvette linkage is mounted to the frame—which means that it doesn't have to be rubber isolated to avoid rattles and vibrations. So you get solid shifts but no lever buzz. The shifter is also adjustable for a shorter throw.

They may have in the braking department, however. Corvettes have extremely powerful brakes and three of the four test cars easily lived up to expectation. But the fourth—the nose heavy, air conditioned, all iron 454—preferred to lock up its rear wheels early and could pull only a little over 0.8G and still maintain good directional stability. No brake system proportioning valves are used in the Corvette and although there is a considerable weight distribution variation between models, Duntov is convinced that none is necessary—but he planned to recheck the nose heavy car situation on his return to Detroit just to make sure.

When it comes to handling, the variables are even more complex. According to Duntov, production cars can range all the way from 0.75 to 0.85G on the skid pad. The 454s are usually better because those models have a rear anti-sway bar which makes them almost neutral. But you can't count on it. There is a considerable variation in suspension rates: up to 10% in the springs and nearly as much in the anti-sway bars—they can't be produced to tolerances closer than that at a reasonable cost. And then there are the tires. For all considerations that make a good street tire—directional stability, ride quality, noise, etc.—the Goodyears are slightly better but the Firestones will usually generate a fraction more lateral force on the skid pad. Then there is car weight, which varied in this test from 3370 to 3675 lbs., and weight distribution. In this test the lightest car, the LT1, turned out to be best, circulating around the pad at 0.80G. It also had the least understeer.

But on the road course it was almost impossible to feel the difference between the four versions. All of them understeer slightly—just the right amount in our opinion—and are extremely tolerant of driver technique. For those who intend to race there is an optional heavy duty suspension but it is so hard that Duntov doesn't think anybody could stand it on the street. And to discourage the masochists, he has fixed it so that you have to special order a heavy duty car—intended strictly for racing, with heavy duty brakes, clutch, rear end, etc.—and not a single convenience option, not even a radio, is available on that model.

It's all a part of Duntov's loyalty to Corvette drivers. He wants them to have what they need—as opposed to what they think they need—in an extremely high performance road car. Because of that desire he frequently finds himself at odds with the stylists. The deluxe wheel cover option is a case in point. The Turbo-Flash styling adds 28 lbs. to the car and makes it impossible to dynamically balance the wheels. Duntov recommends the base hub-cap-and-trim-ring setup. And there have been even more serious conflicts over the basic body shape. Originally the stylists had a big spoiler slated for the rear of the current Corvette before it went into production. Duntov insisted that it be trimmed down to its current non-functional size. Testing had shown the spoiler pushed the rear down so hard that the nose came up, causing the front end to go light—far worse than no spoiler at all.

Occasionally you find a problem that hasn't been fixed. On the 140-mph pass through Nevada in the LS5 we discovered that it would only run wide-open throttle for a few miles before it would overheat. When the subject came up later Duntov nodded—he knew it. It's because of the radiator shroud. You have to have it at low speeds so the fan will be effective but at high speeds it sort of corks off the flow of air that would otherwise be rammed through the radiator. He has the solution on the shelf—a shroud with flaps that open at speed—but the bean counters aren't too interested in that. And since it's not a safety consideration, there is no reason to press the issue. Duntov knows about discretion. It comes with age.

Which is a subject he doesn't talk about much. He's close on sixty and it is weighing on him. But it doesn't stop him. Seemingly, nothing can. You see it when he drives. A few laps at the photographer's insistence—just to finish off. Never mind that it's just to use a roll of Tri-X. It's done right. Wide open throttle till the last millisecond—brake late—brake hard—on the power early. Not a twitch in the line. Just a taste of tire smoke filters through the cockpit. Hell. Zora Arkus-Duntov will still blow the doors off 98% of the guys that buy his cars. And that bodes well for next year's Corvette.

●

NORTHWEST PASSAGE

On the way to Alaska, the first
4000 miles are the easiest.

TEXT BY BROCK YATES/PHOTOGRAPHY BY JIM WILLIAMS

Friday: Northbound, into the wind that drives a cold drizzle across Metropolitan Toronto, shrouding its bold new buildings in dingy curtains of gray. The six-lane highway is filled with random squadrons of traffic, hissing ahead at 75 and 80 mph. Our Corvette—a bleached white, factory-fresh '76—loafs past them, stable and silent, its low-pressure engine pulling 3500 rpm at 90 mph. Soon the highways will empty and the vastness of Canada will come into clearer perspective. The route to Alaska stretches more than 4000 miles, first through the wooded highlands of the Great Lakes, then chasing the horizon across Saskatchewan and Alberta until the Canadian Rockies appear in the distance. From there, it is 1100 miles of two-lane dirt road. Special dirt. The legendary dirt and dust and mud of one of the last great, primeval thoroughfares. The wilderness boulevard of dreamers and fortune hunters and runaways and outcasts heading, as they like to say, "north to the future"—the Alaska Highway.

We move north and west in steps, first jogging around the east end of Georgian Bay, then crossing the sheer walls of the French River, where for two centuries audacious French *coureurs de bois* and *voyageurs*, Jesuits and Franciscan priests—Champlain, Radisson, Marquette, Joliet, La Salle—paddled westward in search of furs and converts to Christ. The foaming rapids that spilled the waters of Superior into the lower Great Lakes are regimented in the orderly steps of the Soo Canal locks, an integral link in the St. Lawrence Seaway system. Where half-wild Frenchmen once mingled with Stone Age Hurons and Iroquois in jittery dramas of treachery and death, now plump, fresh-faced Canadian youths dispense Big Macs beneath the Golden Arches and cruise the asphalt clearing in noisy Camaros.

Saturday: East of Superior, where nature is unchallenged. A single main road, Trans-Canada Route 17, violates the wilderness. Copilot Jim Williams rolls cautiously through the heavy morning fog. A sign warns of a moose crossing, and it is not in jest. A few yards ahead in a misty hollow, the satiny black bulk of a bull moose lies at the roadside, his rack of antlers cocked against the steel guardrail, his eyes cloaked in death. Standing by is an Ontario Provincial Policeman and the driver of a crippled White Freightliner.

The highway is a collection of smooth bends sweeping through stands of birch and aspen punctuated by towering, rocky cliffs that fall away to the lake. The sun is probing through the fog, and Superior, unruffled by the wind, stretches to infinity like a vast, polished marble cathedral floor. Miles pass in groups of 10s and 20s before we see any signs of humanity—generally a camper-pickup topped by a canoe or a set of moose antlers, or a tractor-trailer chugging up one of the long grades. The road begins to hug the shore, which is a rough-cut outline of steep coves and wide bays that yawn toward clusters of wild, rock-bound islands.

We are enveloped in a cloud of noxious yellow smoke. Repelled by the putrid odor, we scramble to shut off fresh-air vents and seal the windows. Drifting across the forests and eddying among the boulders is the exhaust of the Kimberly-Clark paper mill in Terrace Bay, Ontario, one of a number of immense industrial operations that foul the purity of the Canadian wilderness. At its vilest, Newark, New Jersey has never smelled so bad.

We have traveled 1000 miles, and we are still in the Province of Ontario. The long vistas, the clusters of pines and the stony hills begin to look like northern Arizona. Finally the land flattens; the Great Plains lie ahead. A kid in a gas station warns us that Manitoba is heavily patrolled by Mounties in radar-equipped cars. Williams and I agree that we would be honored to be arrested by one of Canada's fabled Royal Canadian Mounted Police. Three hours later, we are obliged. Williams is stopped for 80 in a 60-mph zone by an RCMP officer considerably more mundane than our visions. No scarlet tunic, no spirited stallion, no sled dogs, no Winchester—just another pleasant, efficient policeman doing his job in a pastel-green Galaxie.

The open, agricultural flatness around Winnipeg gives us time to ponder our automobile and its uncertain capabilities. Corvettes are boulevard sports cars—"image cars" in GM's term—intended for short-haul, semi-serious motoring. My own objections about its vivid deficiencies as a legitimate GT have been voiced before, but I'm about to get the opportunity to live with a Corvette in truly demanding circumstances. A Chevrolet engineer, dealing in the kind of candor that is almost becoming common in Detroit, has told us: "Let's face it, the Corvette is three feet too long and 800 pounds too heavy.

The Highway may
be the one road in North
America that lives
up to its claim of being
"world famous."

Nobody in the Corporation has taken it seriously for five years simply because we've been able to sell all we could build without trying. So the seats are awful and the rear suspension does weird things. But within the next two years you're going to see a serious effort to make the car better."

Its weaknesses notwithstanding, we are going to try to drive this boulevard beauty to Alaska over what sober people claim to be the roughest main road in North America. The Corvette's underbelly vitals have been shielded by steel plates; its suspension raised to clear ruts and rocks; its wheels shod in sturdy, high-traction Dunlop patrol tires. But it remains a city slicker in an increasingly rural and a hostile environment. Taking this car up the Alaska Highway had a crazy appeal when first the idea arose, but now as the roads roughen and the skies begin to smear with dark, low-running nimbus formations, apprehension begins to overwhelm amusement.

The car is untested in the ruler-straight marathon of four-lanes that carry us westward. Then another Corvette appears, a shimmering blue L-88 driven by a DNF in an Omar Sharif look-alike contest. He whistles past on the smooth stuff, then angles into a rough detour that parallels the expressway like a railroad right-of-way. We follow Omar as he tries to maintain his pace, but his Corvette is leaping and bucking, its rear wheels fluttering crazily, sparks and smoke oozing from various parts of the suspension. Awful messages arrive through his steering wheel and seat cushion, and he gives up. Untrou-

bled by the same lumpy surface because of an additional two inches of suspension clearance cranked into our Corvette, we nip by him at a steady 80. Chastened by this gesture, he falls obediently into our van. (Someday, somebody will examine seriously the pecking order of the highway and perhaps bring reason to the arcane rituals wherein one driver will pass or not pass another, based entirely on gestures and signals of subservience or supremacy.)

Sunday: We chew at the miles, gulping them in 100-mph gobs, but the vastness of Saskatchewan and Alberta creates a treadmill of rolling plains, broken only by stark, wind-battered villages huddled around the grain elevators that line the Canadian Pacific tracks. We seem mired in a Gobi of waving grass until the towers of Edmonton peek over the horizon.

It is an immense city, unabashedly new and expansive—a sort of Dallas of the north—pulsing with neon, its future carved in pre-formed concrete and stainless steel. For one imagining this place serving as a stockaded outpost on the edge of the Canadian frontier, the illusion is battered away amid the swirling traffic and palisades of motels, fast-food joints and auto dealerships that line its streets. Canada is a nation of roughly 30 million people, most of whom seem to be clustered in four mega-cities; Montreal, Toronto, Vancouver and Edmonton. Where are all those hearty, fur-wrapped Canadians of the deep woods we read about? Lined up at stoplights in downtown Edmonton, apparently.

It is a small green sign beside the busy road, but it is an important measure of our progress. It directs us to a turn northward, north toward the Alaska Highway. The jumble of Edmonton is behind us now, and the forests of pine and aspen thicken until they blanket everything except the thin scar of the highway.

The land is getting meaner. The houses are rough boxes of wood and tarpaper, dulled and tormented by nature. The ducks are fleeing south. Rain squalls, black and burly, move over the forests. Small clearings bear testimony to courageous efforts to grow wheat or forage for scrawny herds of beef cattle, but the wind, driving rain and snow grind down on men without remission. And always at the edge of endeavor is the forest, nibbling, encroaching, an impatient landlord as ready to replant as the jungles of the Amazon.

It begins at a milepost in the center of a sprawling, motel-dominated town called Dawson Creek: the road they call "The Highway." A sign formalizes the moment: "You are now entering the world-famous Alaska Highway." Flags of Canada, the United States and the Province of British Columbia are mounted over a marker indicating that Fairbanks, Alaska lies 1520 miles to the north and west.

The first 83 miles are normal two-lane asphalt meandering through woodlands. We have run a reasonably relaxed 900 miles on this day, and as the northern night deepens, we seek lodgings at Fort St. John, originally settled as a Northwest company trading post in 1798 and once the tramping ground of the greatest of all explorers of the Canadian west, Alexander Mackenzie. Today it is a locus for natural gas and booming agriculture. The wind stings as we unload the Corvette, but there is no snow. Our compatriots back East are convinced that we are a motorized Donner Party, headed for frozen oblivion in a white hell, and much talk and preparation at the *Car and Driver* offices has been devoted to survival in Arctic weather. We think of this on the sixth floor of our plush

28

motel when the horizontal hold on our TV set begins to roll blindly. "I knew it was going to be rough," says Williams, "but I never imagined it would be this bad. Forty miles on the Alaska Highway and already the color television goes wonky."

Monday: The authentic Alaska Highway begins 41 miles north of Fort St. John. There on a gentle slope lies a stretch of narrow dirt road winding out of sight through a stand of aspen, looking for all the world like a brief detour or a short driveway into a Pocono summer home. The mind resists reality, struggles against the hard fact that this dirt road is *one thousand, one hundred and thirty-eight miles long*—as if we were about to embark on the drive from New York City to Daytona Beach, Florida or from Los Angeles to Portland, Oregon. We roll the Corvette onto the dirt tentatively, like a swimmer toe-testing chill water. We have heard the war stories about this road—the choking dust, the rocks and ruts, the mud, the rain and snow, the precipitous drop-offs and the desperate loneliness of the place—and we are overcome by a moment of misgiving. A Jeep Wagoneer appears, headed south. Its headlights (which the law requires be on at all times) glow through a fascia of crusted brown dirt. The machine looks mean and purposeful, a hard-muscled cousin to those shiny, housebroken versions that frolic on gentle dunes in the AMC advertisements. Eyes peer through the cracked, dirt-smeared windshields, dull and fatigued, only to brighten at the sight of salvation—pavement ahead!

The Alaska Highway is like the little girl with the curl: When it is good, it is very good; when it is bad, it is very, very bad. We have been introduced when it is good. The dirt is soft and punky, like a perfectly prepared dirt track, and the corners, which switch back and forth with no apparent reason, are banked. The roadbed is essentially unchanged since the hectic months in 1942 when 11,000 Canadian and American troops and 16,000 civilian construction workers flogging 7,000 bulldozers, graders and trucks punched a road through this wilderness in answer to the threat of a Japanese invasion of the North American mainland. Dodging vast fields of treacherous muskeg (which accounts for much of the aimless curving), slicing through mountain ranges, building 133 major bridges and felling millions of trees, this army of pick-and-shovelers created an overland link to Alaska in nine months and six days.

The day is warm and sunny, and the surface is amazingly smooth. The Corvette can be flung through most corners in third gear, with second needed only on the tightest of the lot. Some straight stretches allow bursts of 80 or 90 mph in fourth. The banking permits a kind of rhythm to be established, and soon we are bustling along at substantial speeds, averaging nearly 65 mph. The road is almost vacant. We zoom past isolated cars—Oregon dopers doddering along in a ragged Ford van, a couple in a Valiant from Montana running as if their trunk is full of TNT, a Volkswagen and several of the battered Dodges and Chryslers that seem to be favored by the locals. Monster trucks appear rumbling past at inde-

Staring straight
in the face of the Canadian
Rockies, you need
more than a little faith
in your machinery.

> The road twists and
> dives through the mountains.
> Amid all this splendor,
> man can only cling to life
> by his fingernails.

cent speeds—cabover KWs, Peterbilts, Transtars, all being driven through the corners like Modified Stock cars.

We have heard talk about the expertise of the Alaska Highway truckers but have not been prepared for the visual jolt of cresting a hill on a rutted dirt road barely two lanes wide only to be confronted by a 60-foot Diesel 18-wheeler rushing toward us at 70 mph. They operate with the kind of intelligent abandon that comes with the knowledge that they will pay for their own mistakes. The piles of wreckage lying at the bottom of deep ravines are proof that The Highway does not tolerate incompetence or imprudence. There are no cops hovering behind bushes like scolding headmasters, no guard rails, no stoplights, no speed-limit signs, no ambulance-chasing lawyers yelping "whiplash," no external rules whatsoever. The government of British Columbia maintains this sparse roadway as well as it can, but safe travel is up to the individual driver. Mistakes can be ugly and deadly. Help is far away. It is conceivable that one could fly off a bend into the bush and lie there until he got better.

It is a revelation to see how much this primitive situation fine-tunes one's awareness behind the wheel. To be as attentive as the typical motorist driving in the sanitized environments of the U.S. would mean certain disaster on the Alaska Highway. Here you pay attention or pay the price. Could it be postulated that the quality of driving increases in direct proportion to the difficulty of the roads?

The Minaker River lies in the middle of a wide valley possessed of that peculiar, haunting stillness that tugs with mystic persistence at the senses in remote, high places. We are at 4000 feet and climbing. Away to the northwest, beyond a dark stockade of foothills, are the enamel-white crests of big peaks. It is the main range of the Canadian Rockies, where this road soon will wind.

Animals are everywhere. Eagles loaf on thermals while Canada jays putter on the slopes. Coyotes wander like stray dogs, and there suddenly is a bull moose eyeing our passage from a small clearing. He is elephantine, majestic, unperturbed. He turns, looking slightly bored, and then jogs into the bush with surprising grace. Is it possible that people shoot these beasts, displaying their antlers as relics of mortal combat, these great forest cows that watch traffic at the roadside?

The rivers of Canada are staggering in their magnitude. Ignored by geography teachers but celebrated by nature, these broad, clear streams swirl with muscle and purpose northward toward the Bering Sea and the Arctic Ocean. The Peace (1054 miles long, 900 feet deep in places), the Teslin, the Tetsa, the Trout—all pure, untouched, perpetual. Who has ever heard of the Laird? Yet its sight is overpowering as it presses for hundreds of miles through the mountain troughs.

The mountains are rising around us, their peaks glazed with snow. The road twists and dives, making tormented headway around the bulging granite mounds. Amid this splendor, man clings by his fingernails, cowering against the next blizzard or savage blast of wind. Muncho Lake, Fireside, Lower Post—these are places on the map. One imagines plucky villages, sturdy places, full of log houses, notched and chinked against the cold, with warm hearths and steaming food for the haggard traveler. Not so. They are bent and tiled gas stations with

a few junk cars and outlying shacks acting as dormant sentries against the forest. It is not uncommon to drive 50 miles through total wilderness only to find an eagerly anticipated destination no more than one man's collapsing, deserted, windswept dream of cohabitation with the eternal forces that swagger through these parts. No one *lives* in these big mountains; one only makes extended, timorous visits.

Tuesday: We have arisen before 5:00 a.m. in the Belvedere Motel. This ungainly two-story structure, enclosing guest rooms, saloon, a bus depot and a Chinese lunch counter, is the biggest hostelry in Watson Lake, Yukon Territory—which boasts of being the second-largest settlement on the entire Alaska Highway. Watson Lake has a permanent population of 511 people.

Heavy rain bores down out of the blackness. A few spots of light glow along Watson Lake's single street, revealing the mud-covered hulks of vehicles stopped for the night. Semis, campers, four-wheel pickups, a few big American sedans—all coated with this special brand of Yukon mud: Wet, it is sloppy

(Continued on page 72)

NORTHWEST PASSAGE

(Continued from page 31)

as wallpaper paste; dry, as hard as cement. Rain can turn the road surface into a rink of gooey mud six inches deep. More than a few hours of hard rain can make the highway impassable.

The Belvedere's lobby, which doubles as the waiting room for the bus that stops twice a week, is occupied by three all-night revelers. The night clerk, a toothless, barrel-shaped woman, swigs on a bottle of Tartan beer. An old boy, thin as a sapling, teeters uncertainly on a bench. His shaggy hair and thick beard is frost white, and his eyes, even at this hour, shine like spring water. A companion, years younger, is solidly built, his nondescript face capped by an immense, Tom Mix-style Stetson.

"Which way you boys headed?" asks the old man.

"North. To Alaska. By the way, how do you think The Highway is going to be with this rain?" we ask.

"That damned road. You can't never tell," grouses the fat woman as she fumbles for our bill behind the counter, slipping an issue of *Penthouse* out of sight in the process. "This summer it washed out at Blazing River for two weeks. You should have seen this place. People sleeping on the floor, people sleeping everywhere. Two years ago, it was shut for three weeks. That was even worse."

"There ain't no work up there in Alaska," says the Stetson.

"We aren't looking for work," we say.

"Hell, they can't even take care of their own people, much less everybody headin' up that way," adds the old boy, sipping unsteadily from a paper cup.

"That damned pipeline. Everybody thinks they're going up there and get rich. You oughta save yourself the trouble if you're lookin' for work," repeats the Stetson firmly.

"That's no problem with us. We aren't looking for work," we say again. The two men slouch back, reeling slightly, puzzling over our mission.

"If you're not lookin' for work, why bother?" asks the old boy.

"Just going to have a look around. In fact, we want to get back through here before the snow flies."

"You've got a few weeks," says the fat lady. "Fact is, you picked a pretty good time to come through. June and September are about our only good months. The summers are dust and flies and mosquitos, and the winters . . ." She pauses, shaking her head at the

(Continued on page 74)

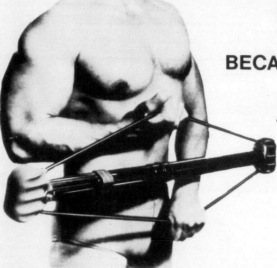

74

NORTHWEST PASSAGE

(Continued from page 72)

magnitude of the thought. ". . . imagine this place when it's 73 below out there."

"Ain't none of it good. That's why you're crazy going up to Alaska. Ain't a spot of work," says the Stetson. He refuses to believe that two able-bodied men would make a trip to Alaska unless they were seeking work. We leave him, his rancor increasing about our elusive talk, while the fat lady begins to maunder about the coming winter. The old man has gimped off toward the bar.

We grope through the early-morning darkness, the mud-smeared beams of our quartz-iodine headlights suggesting a road ahead that looks like a freshly cultivated field. The Corvette is yawing along in second and third gear. The darkness shrouds us totally, creating the impression of being encapsuled in deep space. Dawn comes, a gloom of diffused gray light. We get stuck briefly, but Williams manages to claw the Corvette free before help is needed.

This ocean of forest is beginning to prey on our minds. Texans may brag about the openness of their state, but compared to this place, West Texas looks like downtown Calcutta. Our sense of movement is stunted. The initial delight of running on dirt when it was smooth and dry has given way to depression and frustration that hundreds of miles of switchbacks and humps and serpentine curves, crawling around brooding mountains and wandering through trackless timberlands, are ahead. It is hard to comprehend the mental state of men who once *walked* this way, scratching through these thickets at the rate of a handful of miles a day. What has our speed done for us? Beside create urges for more speed.

We will run for 80 miles along the shore of Teslin Lake, once a backwater route to the Klondike Gold Rush, then cross the monster Yukon River—2000 miles long and the world's fourth largest navigable waterway. We have traveled 3880 miles, yet our only tangible destination is Whitehorse, Capital of the Yukon Territory, a Gold Rush relic booming once again after 70 years of slumber. Then another day in the shadows of the St. Elias Range and we will inch our way into Alaska—a measurement of time and distance that lends dimension to our anthill struggles in the face of Nature. ●

Part II of Northwest Passage *will appear in the March issue of* Car and Driver.

Getting there is half the fun. The other
half is getting back—Part II of the adventures
of our intrepid Alaska-by-Corvette duo.

TEXT BY BROCK YATES/PHOTOGRAPHY BY JIM WILLIAMS

NORTHWEST PASSAGE

46

Wind, carrying frozen farewells from the great mountains of western Canada, boosted us eastward. The roads were flat and transit-straight, and the easy lope of the *Car and Driver* Yukon Corvette across the smooth macadam counterpointed the endless hours we'd spent bucking along the Alaska Highway. The effortlessness of it all brought definition to our gratitude that finally, mercifully, that muddy, rutted, serpentine scar on the wilderness was behind us. Jim Williams and I were homeward bound, in the van of plunging temperatures and low-flying clouds pregnant with snow. We'd left New York 6000 miles and 10 days ago when we'd naïvely but enthusiastically set out for Alaska in our specially prepared Corvette to test both North America's most brutal highway and Chevrolet's fiberglass *boulevardier*. With a mere 3000 miles of Canadian wheatfields and wilderness left to go, there was time to contemplate our brief encounter with the incredible Northwest and what it all meant.

Overwhelming our thoughts were the deeply etched impressions of vastness; of an infinite wilderness stretching away until the trees seemed almost to replace the hydrogen molecules of deep space—of endless, impenetrable, unknowable, unconquerable masses of nature's preserve. The environmentalists who caterwaul that man-made erosions such as the Alaska Pipeline and the Highway itself will blight the area worse than a vulcanizing plant in a city park should see it. Draw the pipeline's route on a map of Alaska and it looks like a hooligan's rampage across the precious tundra, but the reality of the situation is much different. Alaska's, the Yukon's and the Northwest Territory's geographically indigenous ecosystem totals over two million square miles of forest, tundra and ice. The dreaded pipeline will consume a grand total of 8.2 square miles. *Eight point two square miles out of two million square miles of wilderness—much of it unexplored and uncharted!*

The environmental precautions mandated in the construction of the pipeline are basically sensible, not so much on behalf of the migrating caribou (who, like other wildlife, would have accommodated themselves to the intrusion) but more as a symbol of the recognition that industry must make accommodations with nature in future expansions. To compare the utilization of approximately 0.000041 percent of the land of the Great Northwest to the sack of Rome is bleeding-heart balderdash parroted for the most part by people who've never been west of the Hudson River or north of Seattle.

We dimly perceive the patience of nature in the piddling terms of human clockwork, as in the case of the forgotten, 550-mile-long Canol Pipeline, which was built during World War II from Norman Wells, near the Arctic Circle, to a refinery in Whitehorse, Yukon Territory. It was dismantled after the fighting stopped, and now, a mere 30 years later, nature has nearly reclaimed what was—and perpetually will be—hers. And the same will happen within milliseconds on nature's

clock after the last drop of oil has been sipped from the North Slope.

There are still only a few sizable outposts of civilization in the great Northwest: Fairbanks, presently booming because of the pipeline work; Anchorage, a virtual megalopolis with a population approaching 60,000; and Whitehorse, the capital of the Yukon Territory. We made our entry into Whitehorse like men discovering a Sahara oasis. After two hard days of bashing the Corvette across the Alaska Highway's initial 900 miles of mud and dust, the little town huddled in a rockbound valley of the Yukon River looked like Babylon rising out of the pines. The 13,000 souls of Whitehorse are a splendid lot—hearty, open-faced, hospitable and far more cosmopolitan than their number implies. Being the only town of substance on the nearly 2000-mile trek between Edmonton and Anchorage, Whitehorse has served as a trading and travel center since the Highway was completed in 1942. It is one of those wonderful, distinctive communities—like New Orleans, San Francisco and Vancouver—that seem much larger than they really are. Whitehorse, with its cluster of busy motels, its scattering of really superior restaurants and saloons and the general bustle of traffic through its downtown streets, has a spirit and élan missing in many cities 10 times its size.

About seven miles of the Highway around Whitehorse are paved, giving one a brief respite from the dirt. In hopes of returning a semblance of balance to the wheels and transparency to the windows, we took the Corvette to one of Whitehorse's most glittering examples of civilization—its Robo Wash. The kid manning the clanking fandango of whirring mops and foaming spigots treated the car like an archaeological treasure, his eyes bulging as the gobs of clay were sluiced away. He had seen only one other Corvette in his life, and he favored the notion that ours had not been driven to Whitehorse but had appeared before him in some mysterious combination of hallucination and alchemy.

"We saw you guys fly past us," exclaimed another customer, a youth from Mississippi who was driving his Dodge van north to work on the pipeline. "I said, 'There's a couple of boys who are out to wreck a Corvette.'" Our explanation that the car had been specially modified for the trip did little good; he and the rest of the Whitehorse automotive fraternity looked upon it with fascination during our stay. The Yukon Corvette was the talk of the town. A tiny but enthusiastic cadre of street racers appeared to challenge us. Several well-polished Chevelles and Roadrunners loitered around us, plus a Camaro with a large, stock air cleaner peeking through a jagged hole in the hood. Our 3.01 rear-end gear and snow/mud treads made serious street racing a dead issue, and no one seemed much interested in competing beyond the seven miles of macadam. The confrontation reduced itself to furtive stares and demonstration lunges away from stop signs.

Four-wheel-drive vehicles dominate the Whitehorse traffic

scene. They are almost indispensable machines in the mire of spring as well as the snow of winter. An off-road club, the Tundra Trekkers, is based in Whitehorse, but they and the mobs of snowmobilers have an image problem. "There are plenty of logging trails and mining roads for those guys to run on, but they keep chewing up virgin territory," complained one gas-station mechanic. He had come to Whitehorse after beginning to feel crowded in Arizona, and despite his deep interest in high-performance automobiles, he opposed the use of the wilderness as a motorized playground. "There are places where machines just don't belong," he said, gazing at the distant, rockbound hills.

Like most ice-age car freaks, he maintains that the best

time for driving in the Yukon is the deep of winter, when the thermometer descends to 50° or 60° below zero and stays there. "The roads get coated with a layer of really tacky snow when it gets cold, and a lot of the slipperiness is lost. With the right kind of tires, you can really fly. Yeah, the winter is the best time up here all the way around. No tourists or travelers, just the locals, who tend to get a lot closer without all the outsiders. The cold? It's out there, and you can never get away from it. So you learn to live with it."

A brooding, snow-covered shoulder of the St. Elias Mountain Range blocked the way between Whitehorse and the Alaska border. The Highway jogged along the base of the great piles of stone, which resembled mounds of rusted iron

The Yukon Corvette
carried its coat of Alaska Highway mud
like battle stripes—
the scars of its confrontation
with a world
that nobody had ever designed
a Stingray for.

are his efforts—his buildings, his aspirations, his expressions of creativity—so niggardly, so temporary and so gutted of audacity within their shadows?

We stopped for gasoline at Haines Junction, a scattering of battered houses, creaking motels and cafes cowering in the lovely Shakwak Valley. Earlier, as we'd hurried down a long stretch of relatively smooth dirt, a large, healthy-looking timber wolf had stepped out of the bush and sauntered across the road with all the urgency of a beagle crossing a suburban street. Was this a common thing, to see a timber wolf, we asked the attendant? "Too damn common," the wispy, leather-skinned man grumped. "Somebody decided they were scarce, and now those fool conservationists raise hell trying to protect 'em. Scarce, my ass. Since last year, they've killed 16 of my horses."

We drove on northward with the St. Elias Range in silent witness. Lake Kluane lay before us, midnight blue against a bordering rim of white mountains, deep and chilled with the primeval cold of the glaciers that give it being. On its shore, we spotted a pickup truck parked by the roadside, its driver scanning a steep hillside. Far away and perhaps a thousand feet higher, the craggy slope was speckled with white dots—Dall sheep, a pure-white variety of bighorns that populate the remote mountain ranges of the Northern Hemisphere. The man with the binoculars was headed home to San Jose, California after six months of working on the new harbor at Valdez, the southern terminus of the Alaska pipeline. "I'll be back," he pledged, "They'll be building things up here for the next 20 years."

After the mountains, the lakes and the blatant fierceness of the Yukon Territory, the Alaska border was a bit of a letdown—at least in terms of natural splendors. It was marked by a modern glass and brick structure and the beginning of a superb, glass-smooth, two-lane macadam highway, complete with center stripes, steel guardrails and speed-limit signs. After the elemental nature of the road that had led us through Canada, there was something degrading about the prospect of driving in such civilized circumstances. Alaska, our last frontier, looked like western New Jersey. (Admittedly, we never got to see any of the three-quarters of the state's public roads that are entirely unpaved.) We lost little time in turning back toward the undeveloped Yukon Territory.

The Yukon, where you need a high-powered radio receiver to hear static; where grizzly bears outnumber people and eagles float without novelty in the skies above; where man is a mere visitor stuck to the ground with no more permanency than a tent stake—this was our proper place, though it forced us to ponder the frivolities of civilization as we know it: During our particular passage, a couple of America's favorite celebs, Patty Hearst and Jackie O, were in the midst of one of their periodic headline forays. Disinterest has long since drained my memory of the exact issues at hand, but their names were plastered all over the *Newsweek* that we'd found somewhere. I thought about *Newsweek* and its bustling staff with Patty and

(Continued on page 72)

wrinkled from the heat of a monster forge. The nearest of the mountains probed 11,000 and 12,000 feet into the sky, while in the distance the fierce knife-edges of the highest peaks were silhouetted against the blue. The sun was bright and hospitable, but it failed to subdue the bleakness of the mountains. Far off, a colossal peak, its snow-covered flanks glittering in the sunlight, rose above the others. Stopping for a moment, we got out to ponder the staggering bulk of 19,850-foot Mt. Logan, the second-highest mountain in North America, and to try to let our poor brains absorb the fact that we were viewing an object 80 miles away. Far from being inspirational, one must question the crushing, spirit-lashing effect these stone leviathans have on man's psyche. If it is otherwise, why

NORTHWEST PASSAGE

(Continued from page 49)
Jackie—those feeble, vacant *vox populi* VIPs—and how little it all counted in the context of those mountains. What kind of tally can be run up by a spoiled radical-chic guerilla and a vapid jet-set media junkie against all this natural power? Final score: Nature, infinity; Jackie and Patty, zero. And then, feeling stupid for even contemplating such trivia, we went back to wondering if places like the Yukon and roads like the Highway can ever mean anything to mankind other than as remote acreage where bits of mineral are timorously scratched from the earth.

"This place has no real history, only a future," Jim Williams mused. To be sure, man's presence here has been spotty and without continuity. First they came in scattered bands in the early 19th century seeking furs. Then they greedily contested for gold, and now the prize is petroleum and ferrous metals. But in terms of serious colonizing and the measurable patterns of growth it produces, the Great Northwest has yet to qualify. For this place, there is indeed only a future. When it is considered how man can live in comfort in dense little nations like the Netherlands and Japan, it is apparent that the enormity of the Yukon could accommodate and support hundreds of millions of people by itself. That's not necessarily something to be desired, but it's comforting to know we have that kind of margin standing by.

So we left, rejoicing quietly as we passed through Fort Nelson, British Columbia—the general boundary of what we confidently think of as civilization. Exhausted, we found refuge that night in an Edmonton motel. We had promised ourselves that we would not wash the Corvette again after Whitehorse; that we would drive it home with the special mud of the Highway serving as its battle ribbons. We abandoned the car in the motel parking lot, its sides gobbed with dried clay that made the once-white Chevy look as if it had been raked with a giant spray can of chocolate frosting. It was the ugliest Corvette in the world. It was also the toughest.

The morning brought rain. It slanted out of the west in resolute sheets, warning of the advancing snow. Now we were hurrying. Within 50 miles, the last traces of the prized Yukon mud had been washed away. ●

Part I of "Northwest Passage" appeared in the February 1976 issue of Car and Driver.

CHEVROLET CORVETTE

The same old smile that sells.

• Here it is again folks, the new Corvette, back for the eleventh encore of its 1968 act. The well-known routine is still playing to sellout crowds, lined up around the block waiting for the curtain. Look behind the smiling faces in the crowd and you'll find guys that made it big in the cement business. They're dumping year-old Grands Prix for Corvettes so they can live out high-school dreams before their hairlines go

over the horizon. And women are making up a solid 15 percent share of the audience at last count. Freshly liberated ladies who try the pick-up ritual from the driver's seat of a Corvette find it not so demeaning after all. Everybody wants a ride in the plastic fantastic, and a growing number don't seem to care what it costs.

Meanwhile, we're stuck in the middle at *Car and Driver,* not quite sure what to

make of the hordes outbidding each other for an obsolete sports car. On the one hand, we'd love to be at the head of the line with a fistful of money to spend on America's one and only two-seater. On the other, we'd feel guilty about casting another vote of approval for the Corvette in its present, out-of-date form. About all we can do is wring our editorial hands in despair, and appeal to all the true friends of the Corvette *not* to

PHOTOGRAPHY: HUMPHREY SUTTON

Continued

buy, in the hope that GM will get the message and invest in a redesign.

If one model year could possibly arrive with an eminently resistible Corvette, this has to be it. Last year brought the 25th-anniversary celebration, complete with Indy-pace-car replica, and 1980 will see the first serious efforts toward lighter Corvettes, but 1979 is a non-year on Chevrolet's engineering calendar. Outward alterations include such radical moves as crossed-flag emblems (1977 style), replacing the special anniversary brooches used last year. Roof-panel and back-window moldings are now black instead of shiny, and Limited Edition (pace car) spoilers have become an option this year. Inside, an

AM/FM monaural radio is base equipment, 1978 Limited Edition bucket seats are now standard, and the ignition lock has been reinforced for better theft protection. Somehow, Chevrolet knew we'd all been holding our breath for an illuminated visor vanity mirror, so one has graciously been added (as an option). Mechanical changes include halogen high-beam headlamps that will become standard equipment sometime into the model year. There are still but two engines available in the Corvette, both displacing 350 cubic inches. Base (L48) engines get the L82 low-restriction intake and exhaust systems, a change that raises their output to 195 horsepower. The ''big'' L82 motor is

doled a new electric cooling fan if you buy air conditioning. This part (borrowed from the 1980 front-drive Nova) supplements a new five-blade, engine-driven fan that saps less power, so all L82s produce 225 horsepower, with or without air conditioning. Add in the usual shuffling of interior and exterior colors, axle-ratio offerings, and option mixes, and you've got the 1979 Corvette. Never in its 26-year history has this car so ignominiously borne the stigma of a carry-over.

Of course, the sales guys will tell you it doesn't matter. In 1978, the order hopper was full by March, leaving a half-year's worth of potential customers unsatisfied. GM's assembly plant in St.

34

Gentlemen prefer blondes with red Corvettes.

Louis cranked out more than 46,000 Corvettes last year, and to the best of our knowledge, not a soul bought one for less than full sticker. The more the buyers spend, the less they seem interested in buying real sports cars. Corvette customers opt for automatic transmissions, cruise controls, and power windows in droves. Few seem to realize, or even care, that today's Corvette—the oldest car design in production in America—is still the quickest accelerating, the fastest in top speed, and the best-handling car built on the premises. Zora Arkus-Duntov could be the prime minister of Transylvania as far as they're concerned. What these Grand Prix trade-in customers love is the Cor-

vette's Batmobile look, and as long as it's flashy and accommodates blondes in pink shorts, they're content.

Keeping them content is Dave McLellan's job as the Corvette's chief engineer. This Sloan School of Management graduate cut his teeth as a performance guy back in the Camaro Z28's heyday, and while he does his best to keep the Corvette's power-to-weight ratio respectable, McLellan's primary mission is satisfying the current Corvette buyer hooked on comfort and convenience. Yes, this is a drastic turnabout from the Zora Arkus-Duntov era of Corvette development. Chevrolet's one and only engineering demigod did his best to keep the Corvette a half-civilized rac-

er—not too convenient, but plenty satisfying, with a big-block prime mover stuffed under the hood. The steering wheel was in the wrong place, you couldn't read the heater controls at night, and two six-packs filled the luggage compartment, but it didn't matter. Zora made sure the right things happened when you stepped on the gas.

Big-blocks and Zora Arkus-Duntov have gone away together, leaving Dave McLellan with an eleven-year-old design and at least 50,000 customers who want to buy it every year. He hasn't done much to the exterior, because anything short of a complete repackaging would be a waste of money. But inside, the Corvette's been thoroughly overhauled in the last three years. As long as he's stuck with the car in its present form, Dave McLellan wants to make it as useful as possible.

So far, his efforts have delivered about an equal mix of success and failure. Last year's glass-back redesign was a universally appreciated Good Move. The large rear window freshened up the Corvette's profile, and it also added space and light to help relieve the claustrophobia inside this, the most tightly

Optional spoilers trim lift by 215 pounds and add 1.3 mph in top speed.

coupled car known to man. The steering column was shortened, so you no longer look like a praying mantis behind the wheel. Instrument clusters are more legible, although the molded-in allen-head look seems more appropriate to a Monza than Chevy's ten-grand image leader. We also appreciate the addition of a real glove box, door map pockets, and simplified heater controls.

Unfortunately, this new silver lining for the Corvette also has its clouds. The engineer who designed the windshield-wiper-switch escutcheon has demonstrated beyond a shadow of a doubt that a square peg *does* fit a round hole if it's rammed home with a large enough hammer. And, if you choose to plunk down an extra $365 to see sunlight

through your Corvette's roof panels, you'll find they fit at least a quarter-inch proud of the roofline *by design.* Last on our complaint list are the redesigned seats, in our opinion an abysmal failure.

Of course, this wasn't the plan. The new seats were sold to management on their weight-savings merit, and their molded-plastic design is in fact 22 pounds lighter. The problem with parts engineered down to the last ounce is that aesthetic appeal is oftentimes the first pound to go. The Corvette's seat shells have the throwaway feel of parts molded by Rubbermaid. On the plus side, the design features a hinge point raised several inches to provide a level surface with the rear cargo deck when the passenger seat is folded. This allows you to slide luggage back into the hold smoothly and also provides a long, flat surface if you'd rather tote skis instead of your girlfriend.

So far, we'll give the new Corvette seats a B-minus for appearance and an A for utility. For comfort, they flunk. Our informers tell us that stylists designed the cushions, and once they had something that looked good, the job was sent off to the plant for production.

The way these seats feel, it apparently never dawned on anyone to actually sit in them, let alone wear them on a long trip. What you ride on feels like three fat rolls of foam rubber: one at the midpoint of your thighs, one at the top of your shoulders, and one at the small of your back. It's hardly what you would call orthopedically distributed support. Matching fat-roll side-bolsters squeeze your hips like a Playtex. They're great for sideways location in turns, but they appear to be sized for the Diet Pepsi generation, and the broad-of-beam end up teetering *on* the seat rather than sitting properly in it.

We're told the engineers have been allowed to salvage this mess now that everyone agrees there's a serious comfort deficiency, but the fixes won't appear until 1979 production is well under way. One deficiency that won't be fixed is the total lack of backrest adjustment. With this seat's high hinge point, such a feature (now standard on virtually every economy car from Japan) just can't be made to work.

The same look-good-work-bad disease that's attacked the seats has also infected the Corvette's chassis through its tires. This is the second year the options list has advertised a set of P255/60R-15 Aramid-belted, radial-ply, white-letter tires. These Fat Alberts cost an extra $226.20 over the base P225/70R-15 steel-belted, radial-ply, blackwall rubber, so the natural conclusion is that they're the Hot Tip. Not so. We were advised against ordering the optional tires on our test car—the engineers openly admit their virtue is strictly cosmetic—but we wanted to try them anyway. We agree they add to the Corvette's macho-muscle look, but after riding on them for a thousand miles, we'll

Seats come with the car. Special seat covers are an extra-cost option.

stick with steel belts. The 60-series radials are a lot like unruly kids—they have to be seen *and* heard. The tread has something to say all the time—an incessant whir over smooth pavement, a dull roar over textured asphalt, and a howl if you ask them to bend you through any turn at more than half-g determination. On the skidpad, they start to slide at 0.74 g, which is a far cry from the 0.83 g we left the Corvette at last year. In all fairness, the previous test was on well-worn steel-belted radials, while the 60-series rubber was barely scuffed in, but there should be no doubt in your mind which tire is for cornering and which is for cruising.

A skidpad reveals only part of the handling picture; it was over-the-road driving that proved the 1979 Corvette on 60-series rubber to be a small handful. This car's archaic linkage-booster power-steering system has low on-center precision, and the fabric-belted tires add their share of vagueness in straight-line driving. More caster would help the Corvette's directional stability, according to Chevrolet's tests, but there isn't

CHEVROLET CORVETTE *Continued*

room under the swoopy fenders for more than two degrees. So a long trip means constant corrections at the steering wheel to herd the Corvette down a single lane of pavement.

The wide rubber also accentuates this car's tail-happy twitchiness in transient maneuvers. Pitch it into an entrance ramp, tread lightly on the gas, and the beast jerks sideways every time. Broadsliding can be fun, and the Corvette never really threatens a full pirouette, but it's tough to feel you're doing a tidy job of a turn when the back end does all the steering. Again, it's not just the

With the 60-series tires, oversteer is easy. Just stab it and steer it.

tires' fault, but a compound interaction of a rear suspension fraught with deflection oversteer (side loads steer the Corvette's outside rear wheel away from the turn) and tread rubber that wobbles underfoot like toothbrush bristles.

The 60-series tires' one saving grace is straight-line traction. The mighty L82 engine (225 horsepower this year), backed up with the biggest gear money can buy (3.70 to 1), had all it could do to break these tires loose off the line. Wind it up, snap off a one-two shift, and you're at 60 mph in 6.6 seconds. Even with a fairly green engine, our test car easily buzzed its tach needle smartly to the redline in top gear, or 127 mph. Enjoy these disrespectful bursts of speed while they last, because next year the Corvette must follow corporate mandates with a speedometer that plays dumb after 80 mph.

In many ways, 1979 will go down as a serious dent in the Corvette's prestige, even though the car's still capable of turning in the best performance profile of any American car (disregarding fuel economy). The Corvette is getting loose and lazy in its old age. Its appointment with the downsize doctor has been canceled too many times. We'll be anxious to see the effects of next year's diet, but we won't be really happy with the Corvette until the old girl's been retired. The time has come to pass the crossed flags on to the next generation.

—Don Sherman

COUNTERPOINT

• When I first drove the new L82, I marveled at the improvements. Last year's car was feisty enough, but it was nasty, harsh, and unpredictable. The new car was a pleasant surprise. Then I discovered I really didn't like it so much. I got used to it, and it irked me.

The car rides better now: it's more receptive to bumps in the road and your own hind end. It runs fairly quickly and stops the way all cars should. But this Corvette, in the condition in which I first discovered it, had no use at all for changing direction with more than the slightest semblance of good manners. If the front end wasn't pushing and howling, the back end was skewing itself into twitchy oversteer. The power steering had nothing to report but bad news.

The doorjamb sticker recommends 30 psi for the front tires and 35 for the rears if you want maximum fuel economy. The optional pressures listed are 20 and 26 (!), front to rear, if you're carting around a princess who detects peas under mattress stacks.

Do yourself a favor: kick out the princess and pump up the tires to 35 pounds all the way around. *Then* the Corvette will turn where you point it, and the end that usually points toward where you've been won't be so all-fired willing to point out where you're going to wind up.

Bumping up the pressures turned the L82 into a real flail-around unit, capable of handling full-on throttle and full-on brakes with some distinction, and without the dramatic understeer/oversteer transitions the uneven pressures produce.

So I wound up liking it again because a single, simple alteration allowed us to work together . . . even if it is grossly wasteful on virtually every other count.

—Larry Griffin

Whether by design or by accident, this year's Corvette is the most refined ever. Its road manners have become sophisticated, and its controls have evolved into useful instruments that not only direct forward progress but also respond reassuringly, while relaying all the information you need for driving fast and well.

And though the Corvette's personality has been honed and polished, it's still full of character—in much the same way as the latest Porsche 911s. There's still a rumble in the exhaust, a hint of twitchiness in the suspension, and a subdued orneriness that demands your attention when you hurry. An undercurrent of excitement tingles through the whole car; the beast has been tamed, but its soul is still wild. It all made me want to get in and drive fast, and thoroughly satisfied me when I did. So while everyone else looks ahead to the new high-technology, fuel-efficient Corvette looming on the horizon, I advise you to buy now or forever hold your peace.

—Rich Ceppos

I have mixed emotions about the new Corvette. It was, as all Corvettes have been, fun to drive, especially with the roof panels out and the sun shining in. There is still a vestige of that legendary horsepower to get your adrenaline flowing. And not to forget the car's cachet. There may be tens of thousands of them on the road now, but they still turn heads. The Corvette remains what it's always been, America's dream machine.

But all the good stuff was offset, in my mind, by several niggling little faults that simply shouldn't have been there. Especially considering all the years Chevy has had to massage the thing into perfection. The seats were as uncomfortable as they were handsome, there were raw carpet edges showing around the console, the roof hatches squeaked with a vengeance, and the transmission shifted with what can charitably be described as reluctance. I went away from the experience feeling the Corvette is still a long way from what it can, and should, be.

—Mike Knepper

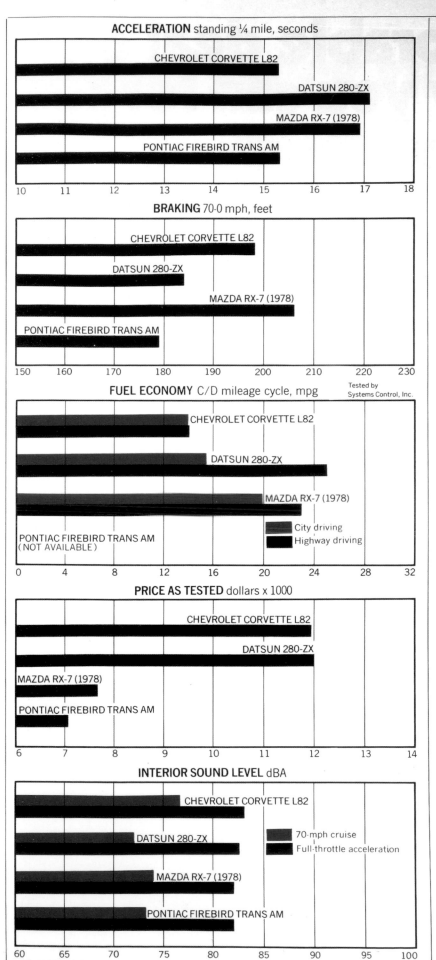

ACCELERATION standing ¼ mile, seconds

- CHEVROLET CORVETTE L82
- DATSUN 280-ZX
- MAZDA RX-7 (1978)
- PONTIAC FIREBIRD TRANS AM

10 11 12 13 14 15 16 17 18

BRAKING 70-0 mph, feet

- CHEVROLET CORVETTE L82
- DATSUN 280-ZX
- MAZDA RX-7 (1978)
- PONTIAC FIREBIRD TRANS AM

150 160 170 180 190 200 210 220 230

FUEL ECONOMY C/D mileage cycle, mpg

Tested by Systems Control, Inc.

- CHEVROLET CORVETTE L82
- DATSUN 280-ZX
- MAZDA RX-7 (1978)
- PONTIAC FIREBIRD TRANS AM (NOT AVAILABLE)

■ City driving
■ Highway driving

0 4 8 12 16 20 24 28 32

PRICE AS TESTED dollars x 1000

- CHEVROLET CORVETTE L82
- DATSUN 280-ZX
- MAZDA RX-7 (1978)
- PONTIAC FIREBIRD TRANS AM

6 7 8 9 10 11 12 13 14

INTERIOR SOUND LEVEL dBA

- CHEVROLET CORVETTE L82
- DATSUN 280-ZX
- MAZDA RX-7 (1978)
- PONTIAC FIREBIRD TRANS AM

■ 70-mph cruise
■ Full-throttle acceleration

60 65 70 75 80 85 90 95 100

CHEVROLET CORVETTE L82

Manufacturer: Chevrolet Motor Division
General Motors Corporation
Warren, Michigan 48090

Vehicle type: front-engine, rear-wheel-drive, 2-passenger coupe

Price as tested: $11,951
(Manufacturer's suggested retail price, including all options listed below, dealer preparation and delivery charges, does not include state and local taxes, license or freight charges)

Options on test car: base Chevrolet Corvette, $10,220; L82 engine, $565; gymkhana suspension, $49; P255/60R-15 tires, $226; heavy-duty battery, $21; AM/FM stereo radio with CB, $439; tilt-telescope steering wheel, $190; rear-window defogger, $102; convenience group, $94; sport mirrors, $45.

ENGINE
Type: V-8, water-cooled, cast-iron block and heads, 7 main bearings
Bore x stroke . . . . .4.00 x 3.48 in, 101.6 x 88.4mm
Displacement. . . . . .350 cu in, 5730cc
Compression ratio . . . . .8.9 to one
Carburetion . . . . .1x4-bbl Rochester Quadrajet
Valve gear . . . . . . .pushrods, overhead valves, hydraulic lifters
Power (SAE net) . . . . .225 bhp @ 5200 rpm
Torque (SAE net) . . . . .270 lbs-ft @ 3600 rpm
Specific power output . . . . .0.64 bhp/cu in, 39.3 bhp/liter
Max. recommended engine speed . . . . .6000 rpm

DRIVETRAIN
Transmission . . . . .4-speed, all-synchro
Final drive ratio . . . . .3.70 to one

Gear	Ratio	Mph/1000 rpm	Max. test speed
I	2.64	8.0	48 mph (6000 rpm)
II	1.75	12.1	73 mph (6000 rpm)
III	1.34	15.8	95 mph (6000 rpm)
IV	1.00	21.2	127 mph (6000 rpm)

DIMENSIONS AND CAPACITIES
Wheelbase . . . . .98.0 in
Track, F/R . . . . .58.7/59.5 in
Length . . . . .185.2 in
Width . . . . .69.0 in
Height . . . . .48.0 in
Ground clearance. . . . . .4.3 in
Curb weight. . . . . .3480 lbs
Weight distribution, F/R 47.1/52.9%
Fuel capacity . . . . .24.0 gal
Oil capacity . . . . .5.0 qts
Water capacity . . . . .20.7 qts

SUSPENSION
F: .ind, unequal-length control arms, coil springs, anti-sway bar
R: ind; 1 fixed-length half-shaft, 1 trailing link, and 1 lateral link per side; transverse leaf spring; anti-sway bar

STEERING
Type . . . . .recirculating ball, linkage-booster power assist
Turns lock-to-lock. 2.9
Turning circle curb-to-curb . . . . .37.0 ft

BRAKES
F: . . . . .11.8-in dia vented disc, power-assisted
R: . . . . .11.8-in dia vented disc, power-assisted

WHEELS AND TIRES
Wheel size . . . . .8.0 x 15-in
Wheel type .cast aluminum, 5-bolt
Tire make and size . . . . . . .Goodyear GT Radial, P255/60R-15
Tire type . . . . .fabric cord, radial ply, tubeless
Test inflation pressures, F/R . . . . .30/35 psi

PERFORMANCE
Zero to	Seconds
30 mph	2.5
40 mph	3.6
50 mph	4.9
60 mph	6.6
70 mph	8.6
80 mph	10.9
90 mph	13.7
100 mph	17.5

Standing ¼-mile . . . . .15.3 sec @ 95.0 mph
Top speed (at redline) . . . . .127 mph
70–0 mph . . . . .198 ft (0.83 g)
Fuel economy, C/D mileage cycle . . . .14.0 mpg, urban driving
14.0 mpg, highway driving

A QUICK COURSE IN THE ANATOMY OF THE WORLD'S BEST PRODUCTION SPORTS CAR.

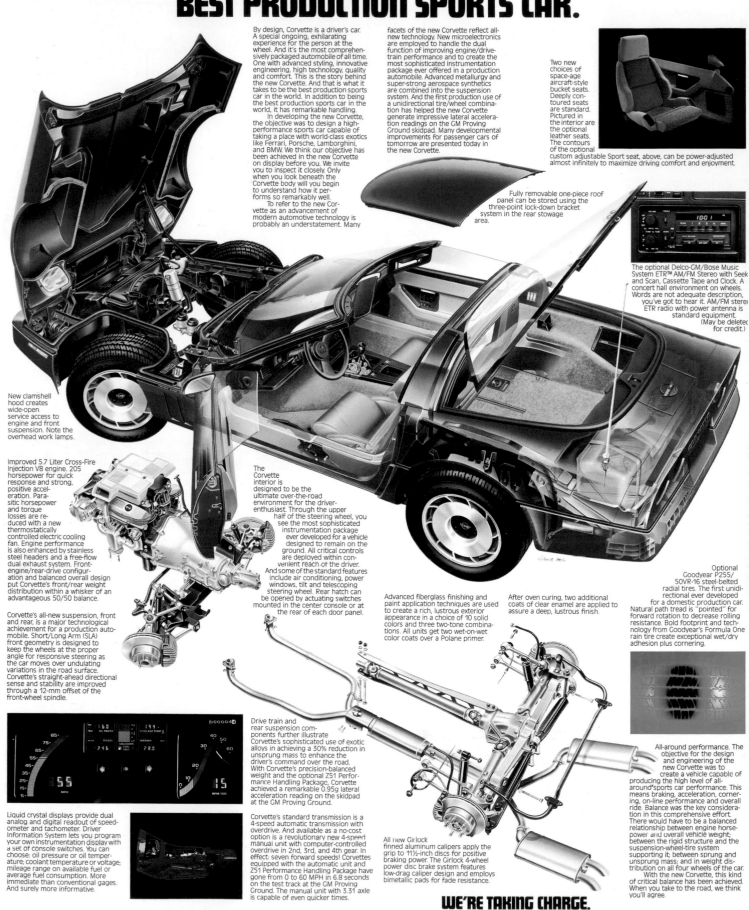

By design, Corvette is a driver's car. A special ongoing, exhilarating experience for the person at the wheel. And it's the most comprehensively packaged automobile of all time. One with advanced styling, innovative engineering, high technology, quality and comfort. This is the story behind the new Corvette. And that is what it takes to be the best production sports car in the world. In addition to being the best production sports car in the world, it has remarkable handling.

In developing the new Corvette, the objective was to design a high-performance sports car capable of taking a place with world-class exotics like Ferrari, Porsche, Lamborghini, and BMW. We think our objective has been achieved in the new Corvette on display before you. We invite you to inspect it closely. Only when you look beneath the Corvette body will you begin to understand how it performs so remarkably well.

To refer to the new Corvette as an advancement of modern automotive technology is probably an understatement. Many facets of the new Corvette reflect all-new technology. New microelectronics are employed to handle the dual function of improving engine/drivetrain performance and to create the most sophisticated instrumentation package ever offered in a production automobile. Advanced metallurgy and super-strong aerospace synthetics are combined into the suspension system. And the first production use of a unidirectional tire/wheel combination has helped the new Corvette generate impressive lateral acceleration readings on the GM Proving Ground skidpad. Many developmental improvements for passenger cars of tomorrow are presented today in the new Corvette.

Two new choices of space-age aircraft-style bucket seats. Deeply contoured seats are standard. Pictured in the interior are the optional leather seats. The contours of the optional custom adjustable Sport seat, above, can be power-adjusted almost infinitely to maximize driving comfort and enjoyment.

Fully removable one-piece roof panel can be stored using the three-point lock-down bracket system in the rear stowage area.

The optional Delco-GM/Bose Music System ETR™ AM/FM Stereo with Seek and Scan, Cassette Tape and Clock. A concert hall environment on wheels. Words are not adequate description, you've got to hear it. AM/FM stereo ETR radio with power antenna is standard equipment. (May be deleted for credit.)

New clamshell hood creates wide-open service access to engine and front suspension. Note the overhead work lamps.

Improved 5.7 Liter Cross-Fire Injection V8 engine. 205 horsepower for quick response and strong, positive acceleration. Parasitic horsepower and torque losses are reduced with a new thermostatically controlled electric cooling fan. Engine performance is also enhanced by stainless steel headers and a free-flow dual exhaust system. Front-engine/rear-drive configuration and balanced overall design put Corvette's front/rear weight distribution within a whisker of an advantageous 50/50 balance.

Corvette's all-new suspension, front and rear, is a major technological achievement for a production automobile. Short/Long Arm (SLA) front geometry is designed to keep the wheels at the proper angle for responsive steering as the car moves over undulating variations in the road surface. Corvette's straight-ahead directional sense and stability are improved through a 12-mm offset of the front-wheel spindle.

The Corvette interior is designed to be the ultimate over-the-road environment for the driver-enthusiast. Through the upper half of the steering wheel, you see the most sophisticated instrumentation package ever developed for a vehicle designed to remain on the ground. All critical controls are deployed within convenient reach of the driver. And some of the standard features include air conditioning, power windows, tilt and telescoping steering wheel. Rear hatch can be opened by actuating switches mounted in the center console or at the rear of each door panel.

Advanced fiberglass finishing and paint application techniques are used to create a rich, lustrous exterior appearance in a choice of 10 solid colors and three two-tone combinations. All units get two wet-on-wet color coats over a Polane primer.

After oven curing, two additional coats of clear enamel are applied to assure a deep, lustrous finish.

Optional Goodyear P255/50VR-16 steel-belted radial tires. The first unidirectional tire ever developed for a domestic production car. Natural path tread is "pointed" for forward rotation to decrease rolling resistance. Bold footprint and technology from Goodyear's Formula One rain tire create exceptional wet/dry adhesion plus cornering.

Liquid crystal displays provide dual analog and digital readout of speedometer and tachometer. Driver Information System lets you program your own instrumentation display with a set of console switches. You can choose: oil pressure or oil temperature; coolant temperature or voltage; mileage range on available fuel or average fuel consumption. More immediate than conventional gages. And surely more informative.

Drive train and rear suspension components further illustrate Corvette's sophisticated use of exotic alloys in achieving a 30% reduction in unsprung mass to enhance the driver's command over the road. With Corvette's precision-balanced weight and the optional Z51 Performance Handling Package, Corvette achieved a remarkable 0.95g lateral acceleration reading on the skidpad at the GM Proving Ground.

Corvette's standard transmission is a 4-speed automatic transmission with overdrive. And available as a no-cost option is a revolutionary new 4-speed manual unit with computer-controlled overdrive in 2nd, 3rd, and 4th gear. In effect: seven forward speeds! Corvettes equipped with the automatic unit and Z51 Performance Handling Package have gone from 0 to 60 MPH in 6.8 seconds on the test track at the GM Proving Ground. The manual unit with 3.31 axle is capable of even quicker times.

All new Girlock finned aluminum calipers apply the grip to 11½-inch discs for positive braking power. The Girlock 4-wheel power disc brake system features low-drag caliper design and employs bimetallic pads for fade resistance.

All-around performance. The objective in the design and engineering of the new Corvette was to create a vehicle capable of producing the high level of all-around sports car performance. This means braking, acceleration, cornering, on-line performance and overall ride. Balance was the key consideration in this comprehensive effort. There would have to be a balanced relationship between engine horsepower and overall vehicle weight; between the rigid structure and the suspension-wheel-tire system supporting it; between sprung and unsprung mass; and in weight distribution on all four wheels of the car. With the new Corvette, this kind of critical balance has been achieved. When you take to the road, we think you'll agree.

WE'RE TAKING CHARGE.
CORVETTE BY CHEVROLET.

CORVETTE COURTESY OF DAVID MAURER AND MICKEY RAT'S VIDEO CIRCUS

Chevrolet Corvette

Four C/D apostles bring home seven revelations.

● Push cinch, Bunko, because this time when we say road test, we mean *Road Test!* We rounded up two production Corvettes, plotted a course that guaranteed a challenging mix of highways and byways, and escaped the office for several uninterrupted days of life with America's hot-dog sports car. Now that the introductory hyperbole has settled, the assembly lines are rolling, and Americans are spending $25,000 to $28,000 (depending on dealer greed) for Chevy's superstar, the time is ripe for taking a serious look at one of 1984's hottest questions: Is the Chevrolet Corvette as great as it's cracked up to be?

In a word, no. But don't be dismayed. If the Corvette lived up to just half its initial hoopla, it would still be one of the most remarkable machines ever to roll down the pike. The fact that it's less than expected is disappointing, but hardly a dead-end deal: Chevrolet is frank about the car's problems, and vast platoons of engineers are inventing solutions day by day.

We picked a pair of Corvettes to test for a number of reasons. Statistically speaking, two would be a far more trustworthy sample than one. A pair would provide front-

row seating for four evaluators. Finally, with two cars we could ride both suspensions now in production: the base system and the vaunted Z51 option. (Our test cars were gold and blue. The red photo car was a privately owned Corvette solicited for maximum graphic tantalization. A lovely piece, isn't it?)

Revelation Number 1: Not a single member of the *C/D* jury cared for the Z51 performance-handling package. For hardware, here's what you get: moderately stiffer front and rear springs, significantly stiffer front and rear anti-sway bars, firmer

year Eagle "gatorback" tires in size P255/50VR-16, so there's no reason to resort to this rock-crusher suspension in search of better rubber.

The problem with the Z51 is that it's a balls-out calibration that ruins the car for day-to-day use. Our blue Corvette with this optional suspension felt perpetually on edge. Really bad pavement sent its wheels bounding, and even minor bumps or irregularities threw the car off on a momentary tangent. The ride was annoyingly harsh most of the time, and straight-line stability was practically nonexistent. In exchange for these hardships, you get lightning reflexes (which we found interesting but un-

shock absorbers, sixteen-percent quicker steering, stiffer lower-control-arm bushings in the front suspension, 9.5-inch-wide rear wheels (instead of the base 8.5-inch wheels), and a few items that have no significant influence on either ride or han-·dling. It should be noted that all Corvettes are now equipped with the potent Good-

Radar Range Revisited

• Old Corvettes were stealthy suckers. Smokey just couldn't seem to see them in his radar beam. In past *C/D* tests, the old Stingray was practically a license to speed: only half as "visible" as a Honda Civic in our radar-range-finding exercise (October 1979), it was, as far as we know, the sneakiest auto on the road. Investigating further, we found that the Corvette's fiberglass body had little to do with its stealthiness. Its secret weapon was actually the fact that its radiator, A/C condenser, and support assembly were tilted back 30 degrees from vertical. This leading wedge of metal apparently bounced the beam toward Mars instead of back into Smokey's receiver.

Now that the old girl's retired, we couldn't resist a comparison. Sad to say, technology has slipped on this critical

vehicle	range in feet
1984 Corvette (frontal area: 19.4 sq ft)	1490
1984 Corvette, headlamps up	1970
1982 Corvette (frontal area: 18.8 sq ft)	1140
1982 Corvette, headlamps up	1300
1983 Dodge Aries (frontal area: 21.2 sq ft	1940
1983 Dodge Ram Van (frontal area: 37.4 sq ft)	3170

front: as our table shows, the new Corvette is significantly more susceptible to radar. Under its hood, the radiator assembly is canted forward twelve degrees (which is enough to discourage radar bounce-back, according to our inside source), but several engine components with vertical surfaces (pulleys, brackets, the air-filter housing) are now exposed. There's also a large, vertically oriented sheet-steel crossmember that backs up the front bumper assembly.

The new Corvette suffers even more when its headlamps are up; our range tests show it's no better than a boxy Dodge K-car. The message: stay out of vans, drive your new Corvette carefully at night, and use that handy shelf above the instruments to mount the radar detector of your choice. *—DS*

CORVETTE

necessary, even during our assault across rural Ohio) and imperceptible body roll.

The test track revealed three more good reasons to pass on the Z51 at order time: our skidpad showed that it doesn't produce higher cornering adhesion (we measured 0.84 g with the Z51 and 0.85 g without), our 1000-foot slalom spotted the Z51 car at 60 mph versus the base-suspension car's 61 mph, and the numerically higher rear-axle ratio that comes with the package delivered no advantage during acceleration runs. The C/D bottom line: the Z51 should be considered the gymkhana package (Chevrolet has used just such a name before on the Corvette's options sheet) for those whose principal interest in life is dodging cones on smooth parking lots.

Revelation Number 2: For plushness of ride, the gold car we tested (without the Z51) was no Cadillac, either. All of the blue car's nasty bad-pavement habits were present and accounted for in the softer-sprung base edition, though the road kick was transmitted through the car much less painfully. Squeaks and rattles seemed more subdued as well.

The sharpest contrast between base and Z51 was not in comfort, however, but in over-the-road handling. To sort the differences, we staked out a back-to-back evaluation stage west of Coshocton, Ohio, that offered a devilish blend of whoops, hollows, twists, high-speed bends, and wide-open straightaways. This fifteen-mile roller coaster was also sprinkled with an assortment of road hazards: creeping, crawling log trucks and farm implements that kept the C/D pilots ever on their toes. All four

testers logged one solo lap apiece in each car, and the result was . . .

Revelation Number 3: The base suspension is the C/D preference for over-the-road handling. Speediness is not the issue, because eight runs over the 30-mile loop proved to us that neither Corvette had much hope of running away and hiding from the other. (Realize that this was *not* a flat-out racetrack fling but instead a real-world comparison at nine-tenths. A slim safety margin was allowed out of respect for all the surprises that can crop up over unfamiliar public roads.)

During these sublimit exercises, the best manners were to be found in the gold base

---

Vettespeak

• Jazz musicians ("cool"), Sixties dopers ("groovy"), and the space program ("A-OK") have all given us their jargon. Today, it's the computer wizards who are interfacing with the lexicon, but the future definitely belongs to the Corvette. Its whiz-bang, Saturday-morning-television approach to motoring is already rewriting the sports-car script. To avoid being left out of the conversation, dig this Reader's Guide to Vette Vernacular.

Push Cinch Derives from the cinch button next to the seatbelt retractor. When you push cinch, you change the inertia reel to a ratchet, locking the belt in place. "Ol' Howie was so scared he about pushed cinch."

Bar A unit of volume inspired by the electrographic gas gauge that shows a full tank as a stack of seventeen glowing bars. "We gotta stop for gas 'cause I'm down to one bar."

Over the Top From the hump-backed graphic tachometer. "We were over the top in third gear and still couldn't shake that Pinto."

Slice of Red The Atari tachometer may or may not be the greatest thing since sliced bread, but its arching trace is, in fact, sliced vertically, just like bread. "Norbert missed second and got a slice of red."

Full Green When the graphic speedometer and tachometer max out, they fill their screens with huge smears of green. "We came over the crest full green, and there was Smokey."

Climb the Fence If the doorsills had barbed wire strung across the top, you couldn't tell them from the walls at Sing Sing. You don't just get into the new Corvette. "Hey, climb the fence and let's go."

Snake Off Used to be that spinning out was the big fear, but the optional Z51 suspension, with its feint-and-dart approach to worn-out roads, offers a brand-new exit line to those who push the limit. "The sumbitch just snaked off."

—Patrick Bedard

Corvette. The blue car with Z51 felt like a numbers-on-the-door escapee from the Mid-Ohio racetrack: it was fraught with foibles that rarely make it into production, the kind that are commonplace in single-purpose racers. The tension through its steering wheel was constantly flicked back and forth by the terrain. The natural rhythms up through the steering and the suspension made it feel as if it was fighting for pole position. It demanded close attention to avoid snaking off (see "Vettespeak") or wriggling out of its half of the highway.

The base car, in contrast, could be driven with ease, all the way from law-abiding-citizen speed right up to the nine-tenths presto pace of the Z51 car. Its slower steering did a better job of filtering out superfluous feedback, particularly on center. Likewise, the concentration level necessary to run quickly in one lane was far lower in the base car. In other words, this Corvette felt like a semicivilized road car with no qualms about being pushed toward its limits.

Revelation Number 4: Genuinely dastardly handling traits are not part of the Corvette, no matter which suspension you choose. Try as we might, neither car could be made to spin out. When forced into corners, each car exhibited a modest amount of predictable understeer. When we did let the tail slip wide or got the least bit out of shape, a touch of reverse lock or a quick lift off the throttle instantly brought the car back in line. And both ends of the car were strongly resistant to bottoming out. As a thrill ride that can also be used as a serious (and safe) challenge to your best driving skills, any 1984 Corvette is hard to beat.

Revelation Number 5: The Corvette's brakes stop the car smartly, but fade can be a problem. The system heats up with sustained hard use, and pedal effort rises noticeably. Chevrolet engineers claim there's really no loss in stopping ability, but over the years we've found it best to slow down when fade is detected in order to keep the heat buildup from permanently damaging pads and rotors.

Revelation Number 6: Horsepower is alive and well in the Corvette. Every one we've driven has been fleet of foot and capable of go-directly-to-jail top speed. The four-speed automatic is also quite a capable tool for generating performance statistics. (The plant in Bowling Green, Kentucky, was threatening to build manual-transmission Corvettes at the time of our tests, but production delays cropped up. Watch this space for a report on life with Chevrolet's computer-controlled-overdrive manual transmission.)

On the darker side, around-town throttle response is jagged in Turbo Hydramatic Corvettes for a number of reasons. The slightest twitch of your toe cracks two

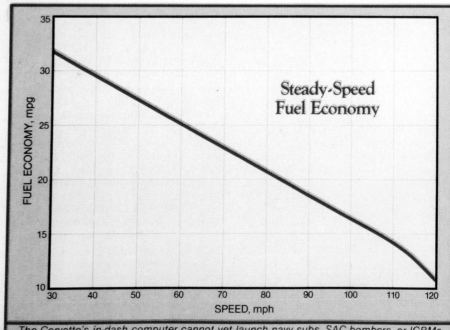

The Corvette's in-dash computer cannot yet launch navy subs, SAC bombers, or ICBMs, but with the proper programming, it can reveal the above steady-speed fuel efficiency.

sizable throttle plates in the twin-TBI system, so there is no way to segue smoothly from a stoplight. Engine output is multiplied so effectively through both the torque converter and the numerically high first gear that the Corvette responds to any go signal by volunteering its own "right now!" into the acceleration process.

On top of this, the four-speed Turbo Hydra-matic has a fairly cranky part-throttle personality in second through fourth gears. It is, after all, a "thinking" device (under microprocessor control), and it therefore takes some time to make up its mind. Corners trip it up most seriously. As you toe into the throttle while exiting a curve, the computer hangs on to a tall gear too long, realizes that you're expecting a downshift too late, jumps to a lower gear about the time you've throttled back in disappointment, and generally stays out of phase with your wishes for what seems like miles on end. Cruising over hilly terrain produces similar headaches: shifts between third and fourth and the locking and unlocking of the torque converter go on like Chinese water torture.

There are, fortunately, several ways to avoid all of this. You can set the cruise control for 75 mph or so, which will keep the powertrain in top cog. You can set the shifter in the third-gear position to tell the transmission to drop its noble pursuit of fuel economy. Or you can wait for the Bowling Green plant to process your order for a manual-transmission Corvette. (It too will be fraught with computer control, but the EPA has kindly allowed Chevrolet to build in a defeat switch to help manage its behavior.)

Revelation Number 7: We know why the Corvette is the way it is. This car was executed by a bunch of engineers with more enthusiasm than they knew what to do with. Their goal—an F-15 for the freeway—has been achieved, and only those with the Right Stuff (driving talent and a kidney belt) need apply. The Corvette is tougher than a fighter plane to get into, and a ground crew is a great aid when removing the canopy or loading cargo through the hatchback. The performance envelope would convince the toughest government appropriations committee. The instrumentation is purposely too futuristic to be appreciated by anyone mired in the twentieth century.

Unfortunately, Chevrolet engineers have not, as yet, had the time to clip back the Corvette's wings for civilians. Such refinement is next on the agenda.

Strange as it may seem, the most fruitful developments in the Chevrolet system generally happen well *after* a new design is in production. This year, the Bowling Green plant is busy building a freedom fighter that's awesome to look at and think about. Next year, if the reengineering goes well, there should be a Corvette we all can love.

—*Don Sherman*

COUNTERPOINT

• The new Corvette is beautiful and powerful, its interior is supremely comfortable, its chassis is devoid of the cheap-think that hamstrings so many domestic cars, and I am absolutely convinced that on a racetrack it can outrun any other production car in the world. By all rights, I should love this car, but instead it leaves me stone cold.

This new Corvette is a deviant machine, a specialist in the dark practice of S-M driving; it pounds, it quivers, it shakes, it punishes its passengers. And that's only one facet of its manifold tortures. It darts, it wanders, and it's upset by any and all road imperfections to a degree that can turn a simple two-lane passing maneuver into a genuine white-knuckle, adrenaline-fired, high-anxiety experience. These evil road manners demand total attention from the driver, while its punishing ride motions do their best to distract him. I don't know whose idea of automotive enjoyment this Corvette matches, but it certainly isn't mine.
                                    —*Csaba Csere*

There's no doubt in my mind that the new Corvette is capable of some impressive feats. I know this because a couple of Corvette engineers kidnapped me for a half-hour one afternoon and took me for a few angry laps around the usually placid ride-and-handling course at the General Motors proving ground. "We'll show you how we develop Corvettes," they growled through clenched teeth.

And indeed they did. We burned through 110-mph sweepers, leaped over simulated railroad crossings at triple-digit speeds, and pounded across chatter bumps the size of small tree trunks. There must have been air under the tires for about half the trip, but the Vette never missed a step.

What this showed me is that, in the hands of an expert driver, on a closed test course he could drive in his sleep, Chevrolet's Corvette flat flies. But that's all it proves, because we civilians drive in a very different environment—the real world.

At least now I know that the Corvette is not the product of incompetence. Indeed, it drives the way it does because the engineers actually designed it that way. Unfortunately, their philosophy and mine couldn't be farther apart.
                                    —*Rich Ceppos*

If Atari's engineers were to build their version of a Porsche . . . no, scratch that . . . if Atari were to do an all-weather Malibu Grand Prix car, *maybe* it would be this much fun. But for now, the Corvette is the best game around. And so realistic. You can read the coolant temperature to the exact Fahrenheit degree. Everything about the cockpit is so George Lucas, from the glow-winkie dash to the g-couch seats. The novelties just keep on coming.

Driving is a blast, too, far better than real motoring. The engine sends little Sensurround power twinges into the seat of your pants at idle and wails as if it were trying to suck in the ionosphere at full throttle. Roaring around is such a thrill, particularly with the Z51 suspension, which launches over bumps and ricochets across lanes like a starfighter run amok. As a way to spend an afternoon, the Corvette beats the *ZingPow-Biff* out of any video arcade.

If this is meant to be a serious GT car, however, Chevy has got to be kidding.
                                    —*Patrick Bedard*

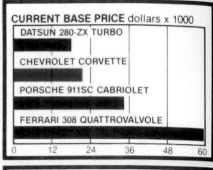

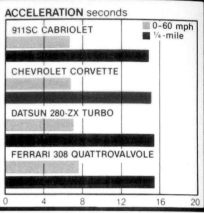

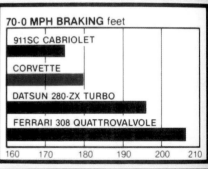

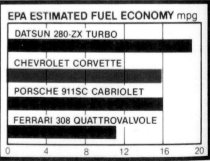

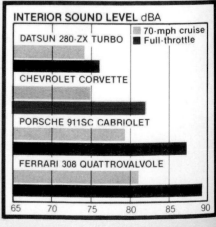

Vehicle type: front-engine, rear-wheel-drive, 2-passenger, 2-door targa

Price as tested: $24,376 (with Z51: $24,415)

Options on test car: base Chevrolet Corvette, $21,800; Delco-GM/Bose AM/FM-stereo radio/cassette, $895; Goodyear P255/50VR-16 tires with 16-inch wheels, $561; leather seats, $400; 6-way power seat, $210; cruise control, $185; power door locks, $165; rear defroster, $160 (Z51 suspension, $600, includes 16-inch wheels and tires).

Sound system: Delco-GM/Bose, AM/FM-stereo radio/cassette, 4 speakers, 25 watts per channel

ENGINE
Type	V-8, iron block and heads
Bore x stroke	4.00 x 3.48 in, 101.6 x 88.4mm
Displacement	350 cu in, 5733cc
Compression ratio	9.0:1
Fuel system	2x1-bbl Rochester throttle-body fuel injection
Power (SAE net)	205 bhp @ 4300 rpm
Torque (SAE net)	290 lbs-ft @ 2800 rpm
Redline	5200 rpm

DRIVETRAIN
Transmission . . . . . . 4-speed automatic with lockup torque converter
Final-drive ratio . . . . 3.07:1 (Z51: 3.31:1), limited slip

Gear	Ratio	Mph/1000 rpm	Max. test speed
I	3.06	8.0	42 mph (5200 rpm)
II	1.63	15.0	78 mph (5200 rpm)
III	1.00	24.4	127 mph (5200 rpm)
IV	0.70	34.8	142 mph (4100 rpm)

DIMENSIONS AND CAPACITIES
Wheelbase	96.0 in
Track, F/R	59.6/60.4 in
Length	176.0 in
Width	71.0 in
Height	46.9 in
Frontal area	19.4 sq ft
Curb weight	3237 lbs (Z51: 3253 lbs)
Weight distribution, F/R	51.2/48.8%
Fuel capacity	20.0 gal

CHASSIS/BODY
Type . . . full-length frame integral with body-cage structure
Body material . . . . fiberglass-reinforced plastic

INTERIOR
SAE volume, front seat	49 cu ft
trunk space	18 cu ft
Front seats	bucket
Recliner type	infinitely adjustable, power-assisted
General comfort	poor fair good **excellent**
Fore-and-aft support	poor fair good **excellent**
Lateral support	poor fair good **excellent**

SUSPENSION
F: . . . ind, unequal-length control arms, fiberglass-reinforced plastic leaf spring, anti-sway bar
R: . . . . ind; fixed-length half-shaft, 2 lateral links, and 2 trailing links per side; fiberglass-reinforced plastic leaf spring; anti-sway bar

STEERING
Type . . . . rack-and-pinion, power-assisted
Turning circle curb-to-curb . . . . 40.1 ft

BRAKES
F: . . . . 11.5 x 0.8-in vented disc, aluminum calipers
R: . . . . 11.5 x 0.8-in vented disc, aluminum calipers

WHEELS AND TIRES
Wheel size . . . . 8.5 x 16 (Z51 rear: 9.5 x 16 in)
Tires . . . . Goodyear Eagle VR50, P255/50VR-16

CAR AND DRIVER TEST RESULTS

ACCELERATION
	Seconds
Zero to 30 mph	2.2
40 mph	3.4
50 mph	4.9
60 mph	6.7
70 mph	8.9
80 mph	11.9
90 mph	14.9
100 mph	19.9
110 mph	25.9
120 mph	36.7
Top-gear passing time, 30–50 mph	3.7
50–70 mph	4.8
Standing ¼-mile	15.1 sec @ 91 mph
Top speed	142 mph

BRAKING
70–0 mph @ impending lockup	180 ft
Modulation	poor fair good **excellent**
Fade	none **moderate** heavy
Front-rear balance	poor fair **good**

HANDLING
Roadholding, 282-ft-dia skidpad . . . . 0.85 g
(Z51: 0.84 g)
Understeer . . . . **minimal** moderate excessive

COAST-DOWN MEASUREMENTS
Road horsepower @ 50 mph	14.5 hp
Friction and tire losses @ 50 mph	7.5 hp
Aerodynamic drag @ 50 mph	7.0 hp

FUEL ECONOMY
EPA city driving	16 mpg
EPA highway driving	28 mpg
EPA combined driving	20 mpg
C/D observed fuel economy	14 mpg

INTERIOR SOUND LEVEL
Idle	51 dBA
Full-throttle acceleration	82 dBA
70-mph cruising	75 dBA
70-mph coasting	73 dBA

CURRENT BASE PRICE dollars x 1000
- DATSUN 280-ZX TURBO
- CHEVROLET CORVETTE
- PORSCHE 911SC CABRIOLET
- FERRARI 308 QUATTROVALVOLE

0 12 24 36 48 60

ACCELERATION seconds
☐ 0–60 mph
■ ¼-mile
- 911SC CABRIOLET
- CHEVROLET CORVETTE
- DATSUN 280-ZX TURBO
- FERRARI 308 QUATTROVALVOLE

0 4 8 12 16 20

70-0 MPH BRAKING feet
- 911SC CABRIOLET
- CORVETTE
- DATSUN 280-ZX TURBO
- FERRARI 308 QUATTROVALVOLE

160 170 180 190 200 210

EPA ESTIMATED FUEL ECONOMY mpg
- DATSUN 280-ZX TURBO
- CHEVROLET CORVETTE
- PORSCHE 911SC CABRIOLET
- FERRARI 308 QUATTROVALVOLE

0 4 8 12 16 20

INTERIOR SOUND LEVEL dBA
☐ 70-mph cruise
■ Full-throttle
- DATSUN 280-ZX TURBO
- CHEVROLET CORVETTE
- PORSCHE 911SC CABRIOLET
- FERRARI 308 QUATTROVALVOLE

65 70 75 80 85 90

Authority

THE 1986 CORVETTE BRINGS YOU AN ENGINEERING ADVANCEMENT UNMATCHED BY PORSCHE 944, FERRARI 308 GTSi, LAMBORGHINI COUNTACH, OR LOTUS ESPRIT TURBO.

Chevrolet Corvette ZR-1

It's out of the park, over the center-field stands.
The fans are chanting, "Chev-ee, Chev-ee, Chev-ee!"

BY WILLIAM JEANES

PHOTOGRAPHY BY TOM DREW

• The Chevrolet Corvette ZR-1, unless we miss our guess, is going to cost some people at General Motors their jobs.

You ask, how can that be? After all, is this not the Corvette from hell? The King of the Hill? The Ferrari-fighting world-class two-seater from the Motor City? A legend-to-be? Yes, it is that and more. But it may still cause heads to roll.

To anyone who's ever been a part of the corporate world, such a situation is familiar. In all corporations, only one person can do *no* wrong. That person is the boss—the chairman or president or chief executive officer or maximum leader or whatever the top man is called. A second group, friends of the boss, can do *some* wrong. A third contingent, those not a part of the power structure, can quite easily commit perceived transgressions against the entrenched moguls. In short, everyone but the boss is at some risk.

Friends of the boss get in trouble by doing something that doesn't work out. The Outs, those not basking in the shared glow of power, get in trouble by doing something that turns out so outrageously well that the Ins become jealous. Once that happens, the Ins will be out for some heads, determined that no one will make *them* look bad ever again.

The whole process of carrying any project—a car, for example—to its conclusion has been reduced to a six-step progression that, once set in motion, is as inexorable as the sunrise: (1) unbridled enthusiasm, (2) sudden disillusionment, (3) total confusion, (4) the search for the guilty, (5) punishment of the innocent, and (6) rewarding of nonparticipants.

But what has all this to do with the ZR-1? Just this: the car is so good that those who didn't want it to happen and those who made it happen anyway have both put their livelihoods on the line. Nothing

this good can come out of a large American corporation without causing shock waves. And we all know what some companies—GM, in particular, has been publicly vocal on the issue—think about anything that rocks the boat. Well, the folks up there on the fourteenth floor had best plan on getting wet feet, because if any car can slosh saltwater over the gunwales of the corporate lifeboat, it's this one.

"If you don't keep pushing the envelope, the limits of what's technically feasible," Chevy's chief engineer Fred Schaafsma told us, "you're going to fall behind." Hear, hear. If General Motors engineering could—or would—improve upon a basic sedan to the extent that the Corvette engineering team improved upon the existing Corvette, the crowds at GM dealerships would cause a nationwide traffic jam.

Dave McLellan, Corvette chief engineer, says, "The ZR-1 makes the statement that we can do things today that no one even dreamed could be done ten or twenty years ago. We've achieved a spectacular level of performance and are still able to meet or exceed all government

standards for fuel economy, safety, noise, emissions, and so on." The ZR-1 engineering team has done nothing less than prove that Detroit can indeed run with the big dogs. The car is, and deserves to be, a source of pride to U.S. enthusiasts.

The new ZR-1 can provide the best driver in the world with all the slam-bam power that he could ask for, yet its personality and demeanor are such that drivers who are less than world-class—a group that, by our observation, includes a great many owners of high-performance cars—are remarkably well protected from themselves.

Does this mean you can't get yourself in trouble behind the wheel of a ZR-1? No. Does it mean that you have to be suicidal to fall victim to its power and speed?

the car we had only driven for a limited distance on the test track. The choice of Europe as an introductory venue permitted us to experience the Corvette in the arena dominated by Ferraris, BMWs, and big, whistling Mercedes sedans—an arena otherwise populated by small, nimble cars that run fast on the autobahns and autoroutes and almost as fast on the twisting, sometimes rough secondary roads. Would this American beast still pound its chest after such an encounter?

Certainly it has the equipment, on paper and in fact, to compete anywhere. To review, the Corvette ZR-1 is a rear-drive sports car powered by a 32-valve, 5.7-liter, port-fuel-injected V-8 engine with an aluminum block and aluminum heads. The engine was designed by GM's Group Lotus Division, was further developed by GM, and is built under contract by Mercury Marine in Oklahoma, a facility with more than a passing familiarity with high-muscle aluminum engines.

The 32-valve V-8 engine, "LT5" on the options sheet, has two camshafts on each of its aluminum heads. Maximum horsepower—achieved at 6200 rpm—is 380. The torque curve shows a maximum of 370 pound-feet at 4200 rpm, and the band feels about as wide as, say, Utah.

The engine's performance is best described as otherworldly. Its power just

Yes. Left to its own devices, the ZR-1 is at once the most exciting and responsible high-performance car ever conceived in Detroit, let alone ever built. It feels glued to the pavement, and it goes as if it were powered by equal parts lightning and solid rocket fuel. It even looks tough, if you stand behind it so you get the prime view of the rear tires—tires so fat that only the differential housing seems to

prevent their meeting in the middle. The ZR-1 is the kind of machine that will send the safety Nazis to their daybeds with the vapors, even as it brings car lovers to their feet clapping and cheering.

The last of the ZR-1's umpteen auto-show introductions (Los Angeles, Detroit, Chicago) took place in Geneva, Switzerland, of all places, and—at long last—involved a long-distance drive in plain warps the mind. The ZR-1 has the ability to take you from 0 to 60 mph in 4.5 seconds and from a stop to 100 in 10.4 seconds. We also recorded a 0-to-150-mph time of a tick under half a minute. Top speed, for the adventurous, is a sizzling 175 miles per hour.

Behind the engine is a six-speed manual transmission that's as sweet as anything mechanical you're likely to lay a hand on. Capable of withstanding 425 pound-feet of torque, the six-shifter is the same manual gearbox used in all 1989 Corvettes, but it's heaven sent for the Corvette from hell.

Zahnradfabrik Friedrichshafen AG, usually referred to simply as ZF, designed the six-speed transmission especially for the Corvette. The fully synchronized unit derives much of its slick operation from an internal-rail shift mechanism and a hydraulically actuated, 280mm-diameter pull-type clutch. Because GM has a severe allergy to seeing the gas-guzzler tax applied to any of its cars, the Corvette team softened the fuel gluttony by installing a system known as computer-aided gear selection. Rich Ceppos explains the system's intricacies in his accompanying Corvette convertible review; we'll just add that the CAGS-equipped six-speed transmission is infinitely more pleasurable to use than the old Doug Nash 4+3 manual overdrive transmission.

Transmission particulars aside, you should know that shifting could not be easier. The clutch-pedal effort is mild, and the gearbox is as at home under city driving conditions as it is on mountain roads taken at speed.

Though the driveline comes from across the water, the exterior remains pure American. There are no significant differences between the standard L98-powered Corvette and the LT5-powered ZR-1. But a close examination of the rear reveals that the ZR-1 is some three inches wider in the fanny, with the smooth flaring-out process beginning at the front edge of the doors and ending in a square-lensed taillamp fascia. The ZR-1 distances itself from its lesser compadres with the kind of subtlety dear to the hearts of Q-ship lovers.

The added width is there for a purpose: to provide shelter for a pair of tires that the word "humongous" was surely coined to describe. The ZR-1 carries 315/35ZR-17 Goodyear Eagle unidirectional gatorbacks in the rear and 275/40ZR-17 Eagles up front. Wheel width is 9.5 inches in front and 11.0 inches in the back.

The only drawback we found with the tires, which are loosely based on Goodyear's Formula 1 rain tires, was an oversupply of road noise. Their benefits, which come in the form of limpetlike adhesion to the earth's paved surfaces, go far toward minimizing the negative effects of the noise. As big as these tires are, we may see bigger yet. Goodyear says that size-405 tires are now practical to build—for the next Corvette, perhaps. Meanwhile, the current tires are protected and monitored by low-tire-pressure warning sensors that light up an alert on the dash whenever any tire's pressure falls below a preset level. The result of a ten-year, ten-million-mile testing program, the low-tire-pressure warning system (option-code "UJ6") can sense variations of plus or minus 1 psi.

Behind the wheels are vented disc brakes developed by PBR Automotive, an arm of Brake and Clutch Industries Australia Pty, Ltd.—yet another group of outlanders. The big 13.0-inch front discs (the rears are an inch smaller in diameter) reflect lessons learned during Corvette Showroom Stock endurance racing and are as good to the touch as any we've set a toe to. The brakes will haul the ZR-1 to a stop from 70 mph in an impressive 170 feet, and fade is not a part of the ZR-1 braking equation.

The suspension is the same sporting combination of Z51 heavy-duty suspension and FX3 selective ride control that can be ordered on garden-variety Vettes. That is, moderately stiff transverse fiberglass springs, thick anti-roll bars, and adjustable Delco/Bilstein gas-filled shock absorbers. The only departure from the standard setup is a thicker rear anti-roll bar, which is needed to cope with the ZR-1's added weight and power and larger rear tires.

Inside all is reasonably familiar, but if you scrutinize the console between the seats you'll see two unfamiliar objects: a lock with a key in it and a three-position switch.

First, the lock, or kiddie key. This gives the operator a choice of full or reduced engine power, sealing off the high-rpm end of the induction system and reducing peak output by about 150 hp. This means that young drivers can be sent to play in traffic with at least some comfort to a parent. The switch has been incorrectly called the valet key—incorrect because any parking-lot attendant unable to cause an owner grief with the 230 or so remaining horses just isn't trying.

The other switch, which operates the FX3 Selective Ride Control system, makes a real difference in the ZR-1—and, indeed, in all Corvettes so equipped. Its three settings—Touring, Sport, and Performance—allow the driver to tailor the suspension to meet variations in road conditions, levels of driver aggression, and comfort requirements. Within each mode, there are six gradations of shock-absorber damping; they vary with speed to maintain a constant level of ride control. The Performance setting will rattle your fillings over rough roads, but the other two are useful in adapting the car to differing roads and driving styles. A rough road can be tamed by switching to the Touring setting, and the Sport setting can draw real cornering performance—and surprising comfort—from the ZR-1 on a smooth, twisting surface. Without the FX3 system, the ZR-1 would not be the grand tourer it is.

We drove the ZR-1 first from Geneva to southwestern France and later from Montpelier to the principality of Andorra, a tiny dot in the Pyrenees Mountains. Altogether, we spent somewhere between 700 and 800 miles in the car. A number of observations resulted. First, the ZR-1 makes every previous Corvette seem antediluvian. It also makes you wonder why anyone would spend more than $50,000 on a two-seater—given that the ZR-1 will be available for about that. But the best news of all is that the Corvette standard-bearer is not some overpowered, noisy (well, not *too* noisy) rattler that feels as if its engine were trying to escape its body.

Driving the ZR-1 reminds you that it is possible to create a car that is bewilderingly fast but that maintains an air of civilization about it. Unlike previous Corvettes, the ZR-1 doesn't subject its driver to corporal punishment in the form of a head-rattling ride quality. Quite the opposite, in fact. Twice, after driving hard all day on French roads that ranged from challenging to hostile, we emerged unscathed and unbrutalized by the ZR-1. This feeling of freshness after a long and difficult drive is stuff of which great grand-touring cars are made.

Twice, once through poor planning on our part, we were forced to stand hard on the brakes. They stopped us short of disaster with the sureness of a racing car. Innumerable times we called on the engine for extra effort in passing situations. The effort was given freely and without incident. Despite the constant stream of brute strength that surges through the seat and into your body, we never had the feeling that we were in anything but a finely tuned example of true automotive craftsmanship.

The car takes mountain turns—*hard* mountain turns—with a neutrality that would do credit to the Swiss banking industry. The clutch action and the shifter throw make power application pleasurably smooth, and the amount of power available, as we've noted, simply exceeds the expectations of sane persons.

Were there complaints? A few. The road noise has already been mentioned, and some of the test cars we drove had considerable wind whistle at both the A-pillars and the C-pillars. After the hard run to Andorra, we finally coaxed some familiar squeaks from the fiberglass body, but nothing that would ruin your day. The garish electronic dash neither pleases nor works properly. Time after time we came to a full stop and waited for the electronic speedometer to catch up—or, more properly, wind down. There seems little excuse for that.

The seats are just fine and can be adjusted to an almost limitless number of driving positions. Even the seat wings and lumbar supports are power controlled. The overall look of the dash and other plastic-clad surfaces stops short of being cheap, but it stops even further from richness. A redo of the interior is due for the 1990 model year, however, so we'll hope for improvement.

Meanwhile, we will lust after the ZR-1. Only a few hundred will be built during 1989, and production—which is limited by engine availability—will likely not exceed 4000 units annually.

Persistent rumors of engine problems, primarily overheating and oil-system malfunctions, dogged the ZR-1 during the first quarter of 1989. Chevrolet denies them categorically, and, indeed, we watched a dozen journalists and engineers flog thirteen ZR-1s for three solid days in France—including time on Goodyear's Mireval test track—with nary a misfire. We're therefore willing to believe that the rumors stemmed from normal developmental teething pains and not from product irregularities.

We're also willing to hope (we'll believe it when we see it) that the ZR-1 will spark other units of General Motors to produce cars equal in their class to the ZR-1. The single-minded effort toward a common goal—performance excellence—put forth by the Corvette engineering team should be an example to the entire American industry. Will the industry follow? We'll see.

Meanwhile, we'll look forward hungrily to more time in the car that, for now, is the best thing yet seen from an American manufacturer . . . and we'll hope that the wrong people at Chevrolet don't lose their jobs because the ZR-1 they created is so good at its job. ●

Vehicle type: front-engine, rear-wheel-drive, 2-passenger, 2-door sedan

Price as tested: $51,500

Options on test car: tinted-glass lift-out roof panel

Standard accessories: power steering, windows, seats, and locks, A/C, cruise control, tilt steering, rear defroster

Sound system: Delco-GM/Bose AM/FM-stereo radio/cassette, 4 speakers

ENGINE
Type	V-8, aluminum block and heads
Bore x stroke	3.90 x 3.66 in, 99.0 x 93.0mm
Displacement	349 cu in, 5727cc
Compression ratio	11.0:1
Engine-control system	GM electronic with port fuel injection
Emissions controls	3-way catalytic converter, feedback fuel-air-ratio control, EGR, electric auxiliary air pump
Valve gear	chain-driven double overhead cams, 4 valves per cylinder, hydraulic lifters
Power (SAE net)	380 bhp @ 6200 rpm
Torque (SAE net)	370 lb-ft @ 4200 rpm
Redline	7200 rpm

DRIVETRAIN
Transmission	6-speed
Final-drive ratio	3.54.1, limited slip

Gear	Ratio	Mph/1000 rpm	Max. test speed
I	2.68	7.8	56 mph (7200 rpm)
II	1.80	11.6	83 mph (7200 rpm)
III	1.31	15.9	114 mph (7200 rpm)
IV	1.00	20.8	150 mph (7200 rpm)
V	0.75	27.8	175 mph (6300 rpm)
VI	0.50	41.6	152 mph (3650 rpm)

DIMENSIONS AND CAPACITIES
Wheelbase	96.2 in
Track, F/R	59.6/61.9 in
Length	177.4 in
Width	74.0 in
Height	46.7 in
Frontal area	19.4 sq ft
Ground clearance	4.7 in

Curb weight	3440 lb
Weight distribution, F/R	52.4/47.6%
Fuel capacity	20.0 gal
Oil capacity	12.0 qt
Water capacity	16.7 qt

CHASSIS/BODY
Type	full-length frame integral with body
Body material	fiberglass-reinforced plastic

INTERIOR
SAE volume, front seat	49 cu ft
trunk space	18 cu ft
Front seats	bucket
Seat adjustments	fore and aft, seatback angle, front height, rear height, lumbar support, upper side bolsters
General comfort	poor fair good **excellent**
Fore-and-aft support	poor fair good **excellent**
Lateral support	poor fair good **excellent**

SUSPENSION
F	ind, unequal-length control arms, plastic leaf spring, 3-position cockpit-adjustable electronically controlled shock absorbers, anti-roll bar
R	ind; fixed-length half-shaft, 2 lateral links, and 2 trailing links per side; plastic leaf spring; 3-position cockpit-adjustable electronically controlled shock absorbers, anti-roll bar

STEERING
Type	rack-and-pinion, power-assisted
Turns lock-to-lock	2.3
Turning circle curb-to-curb	40.0 ft

BRAKES
F	13.0 x 1.1-in vented disc
R	12.0 x 1.1-in vented disc
Power assist	vacuum with anti-lock control

WHEELS AND TIRES
Wheel size	F: 9.5 x 17 in; R: 11.0 x 17 in
Wheel type	cast aluminum
Tires	Goodyear Eagle ZR, F: P275/40ZR-17; R: P315/35ZR-17
Test inflation pressures, F/R	35/35 psi

CAR AND DRIVER TEST RESULTS

ACCELERATION	Seconds
Zero to 30 mph	1.9
40 mph	2.6
50 mph	3.5
60 mph	4.5
70 mph	5.7
80 mph	7.2
90 mph	8.6
100 mph	10.4
110 mph	12.5
120 mph	15.0
130 mph	18.4
140 mph	23.2
150 mph	29.6
Top-gear passing time, 30–50 mph	11.5
50–70 mph	11.7
Standing ¼-mile	12.8 sec @ 111 mph
Top speed	175 mph

BRAKING	
70–0 mph @ impending lockup	170 ft

Fade	**none** moderate heavy

HANDLING	
Roadholding, 300-ft-dia skidpad	0.89 g
Understeer	**minimal** moderate excessive

COAST-DOWN MEASUREMENTS	
Road horsepower @ 30 mph	5 hp
50 mph	13 hp
70 mph	29 hp

PROJECTED FUEL ECONOMY	
EPA city driving	**16 mpg**
EPA highway driving	25 mpg

INTERIOR SOUND LEVEL	
Idle	55 dBA
Full-throttle acceleration	89 dBA
70-mph cruising	74 dBA
70-mph coasting	74 dBA

Predators

Corvette ZR-1 vs. Porsche 911 Turbo:
The horsepower wars continue.

BY RICH CEPPOS

• This is a territorial dispute, a grudge match between two longtime enemies determined to dominate one another—and determined to gain control of the turf they have fought over for years. These are two wild animals sharing one clearly focused purpose: speed. Beneath the skin-tight sheetmetal, their ferocious hearts pound with pent-up power. They prowl the streets like jungle cats.

The Porsche 911 Turbo and the Chevrolet Corvette ZR-1 are predators of the road.

The rivalry between these two models goes back to 1965, the year the 911 first appeared. These two cars have always tried to achieve the same goals—all-conquering performance and handling—but in vastly different ways. The German approach emphasizes Son of Beetle technology: the six-cylinder engine is smaller

42

in displacement, air-cooled, and horizontally opposed, and it's shoehorned into the stubby tail of a compact, lightweight body. Everyone knows the American way: more is better. A husky steel chassis is wrapped in fiberglass skin and stuffed with a massive, front-mounted V-8.

Over the years, the battle for superiority has shifted back and forth, as first one and then the other upped the ante with a variety of strategies: better suspensions, more power, more efficient aerodynamics. This perennial contest has resulted in the two cars you see here, the most powerful versions of the Corvette and 911 ever sold in America.

There is scant dissent that the ZR-1 is the most stupefying Corvette ever produced. In tests it has proved to be a true supercar, but it continues its roughneck tradition—heavy on brute force, dizzying

speed, and race-car handling but lacking in grace and refinement. It's still a wild thing, one of the wildest automobiles this side of a $400,000 Ferrari F40.

Going into this test, the new 911 Turbo posed a number of questions. Its predecessors, sold here off and on since 1978, have had a legendary history of alternately delighting and intimidating their drivers. Their chassis had an ornery streak, their powerful turbocharged engines suffered from hairy all-or-nothing response to the throttle, and their price tags were funnier than Rodney Dangerfield. And, of course, their fat-fendered bodies looked mean enough to make Corollas quake.

This new Porsche, however, is based on the thoroughly modernized Carrera 2 chassis. A perusal of its spec sheet indicates that it should be even hotter than

before: its reworked 3.3-liter flat six is rated at 315 horsepower at 5750 rpm, up 33 hp from the last turbo. It boasts the fattest tires ever fitted to a 911 chassis. Its brake rotors are made from the same high-temperature alloy used on Porsche's 962 endurance racers. It packs an innovative limited-slip differential that not only improves driving traction, but can lock up under simultaneous braking and cornering to improve stability. But is this enough to make it the baddest cat in the asphalt jungle?

To find out, three *C/D* editors embarked on a three-day, 1300-mile, total-immersion experience. Hard driving had to be part of the trial, so we included a large dose of rural two-lane, and we dropped in at a race circuit to let these big cats really stretch out—the better to judge the capabilities of these nasty boys

PHOTOGRAPHY BY DICK KELLEY

43

Porsche 911 Turbo

Highs: Sinus-clearing performance, 180-proof audacity.

Lows: Looney Tunes price, nervous handling.

The Verdict: An awesome dude in a silk shirt.

without worrying about sliding off into Uncle Fred's front yard.

There would be plenty of routine driving too: stop-and-go city traffic and long miles on Midwestern Interstates. After all, even a wild animal of the road is hemmed in by reality most of the time. Would either car be impossible to live with when the pace slowed down?

Our trek began on the Atlantic docks in Charleston, South Carolina, where the Porsche Turbo arrived from Germany. From Charleston we headed down the coast to Savannah, Georgia, home of the Roebling Road race circuit. Roebling's combination of ample straightaways and daunting high-speed sweeps was tailor-made for powerful sports cars.

From there we scratched our way north on the kind of roads they write

44

Chevrolet Corvette ZR-1

Highs: Racing-car speed, handling to match.

Lows: Off-the-rack looks, interior quality needs work.

The Verdict: A wild animal you can live with—barely.

songs about; writhing two-lanes through North Carolina's Nantahala National Forest and the Great Smoky Mountains National Park (which North Carolina shares with Tennessee). We roared through enchanted forests and quiet valleys, past tin-roofed cabins with pungent smoke curling from their chimneys. The long final leg, Knoxville to Ann Arbor, was on mind-numbing Interstate.

But something else happens when you go on a long trip with cars of this nature. Cars like these can change your life, even if your affair with them is short. They confer power and authority and presence upon the driver. People respond differently around them. Things happen that feel extraordinary. You are stared at, examined, considered; the pedestrians wonder who you are. So, all the while, we

45

were on another kind of uncharted trip, the route up in the head.

The effect is mildly narcotic, and it persuaded us to add a special category to the ratings chart that would reflect the mesmerizing effect these cars had on us and the people we came in contact with. We call it the "audacity rating."

Right here, pause and listen to the voice of another editor on the trip:

The convenience-store cashier tells us that Becky's Home Cooking Restaurant is only a few blocks away. But we are strangers, and the signs in Rosman, North Carolina, are not so clear to us Yankees, and soon we have to stop and ask again.

We ask a telephone repairman.

"Bake-ees?" he says, correcting our Northern pronunciation. "Why, it's rayt dahn nair. Isstreet: raytdahnair." So it is, and across the street is an audience: a dozen adolescents digging a drainpipe ditch for their high school. As we rumble toward them, the shoveling stops. Their heads swivel in unison, like deer sensing movement.

As we exit the lot after the meal, our audience is twirling their fingers at us, signaling us to squeal the tires. Leaving positive impressions on young minds is a civic duty, but we hesitate, noting a county patrol car parked up the street. Rich gets on the 911 anyway, but as soon as it heaves forward with boost, there is the officer, walking toward his car. Wheeeeeeechugaluga . . . the 911 lurches back down, and we coast by him at idle, looking straight ahead. Wonder if the kids got their nickel's worth . . . —Don Schroeder

Porsche 911 Turbo
Second Place

If audacity were all that counted, this contest would have been decided before it began. The 911 Turbo is Mr. Universe in a $1500 Italian suit. Its bulging sheetmetal and massive rear wing promise race-car performance. Its flawless bodywork and mirror-like finish suggest images of white-coated craftsmen fitting each part with meticulous care—which is not all that far from the truth. The car looks very, very expensive, which of course it is.

How expensive? Try $105,191. And our car came with just one add-on option: the $891 limited-slip differential. The price does include both the new federal luxury tax and the gas-guzzler tax.

For that kind of scratch, it's at least reassuring to discover that the 911 Turbo is rife with elegant engineering. The suspension's control arms are beautiful forged-alloy pieces. The brake rotors are cross-drilled like a race car's for maximum cooling. Look under the rear

Csaba's Excellent Acceleration Test

• Before we clocked the ZR-1 and the Porsche Turbo, all three writers who participated in this comparison test seemed to think the Corvette was the slightly quicker car. Yet during instrumented testing, the Porsche easily out-dragged the Corvette. Do our writers have lousy seat-of-the-pants feel, or is there something else going on here?

What we're seeing is the difference between track testing and street driving. When we measure acceleration at the track, we do whatever it takes to get the quickest times, short of exceeding the engine's redline, and we don't do any "speed" or "power" shifting (shifting with the accelerator to the floor and giving the clutch a quick, synchronized jab of the foot).

For best results, we usually abruptly release the clutch ("drop" it) at high rpm to spin the tires and get the car moving quickly. The ideal clutch-release rpm is one that lets the spinning rear tires hook up with the pavement just as the engine surges upwards into the heart of its power band.

For cars powered by turbocharged engines, which are usually relatively small in displacement and therefore gutless until the turbocharger spools up, this approach can make for a dramatic start. For example, the ideal clutch release for the 911 Turbo was a tire-smoking 4500 rpm, which yielded a 0-to-60-mph run of 4.4 seconds.

By comparison, the ZR-1 has less traction and much more low-end power than the Porsche. As a result, a relatively non-violent clutch engagement around 2000 rpm produced the optimal start, resulting in a 4.9-second 0-to-60 clocking.

Although the 911 Turbo turned out to be quicker than the ZR-1 by half a second, how many Porsche owners would whip their $100,000 mounts hard enough to prove it on the street? Even aggressive real-world driving relies on starts more like the Corvette's than the Porsche's, and that's why our writers perceived the ZR-1 to be the quicker car.

We've considered creating a test to measure realistic, everyday street performance to go along with the all-out track tests. The problem was developing a moderate launch procedure that we could repeat perfectly day after

day on car after car.

That turned out to be impossible, so we found another solution. Instead of starting from rest, we would initiate an acceleration test from 5 mph with the car in first gear and the clutch fully engaged. This approximates the performance of a gradual launch while eliminating most of the variables.

At 5 mph, the Porsche's 3.3-liter, low-compression engine is turning about 750 rpm and the turbocharger is asleep; consequently there's minimal power. Hit the throttle and it takes about a second to get going before it blasts off, reaching 60 mph in 5.7 seconds.

Likewise at 5 mph, the ZR-1 produces just 625 rpm, but its 5.7-liter high-compression V-8 responds instantly and quickly hits its stride, pushing the Vette to 60 mph in 5.3 seconds and beating the Porsche.

We've experimented with this test on other cars, as shown in the table here. With an automatic transmission, the street-start procedure leaves the transmission in drive and doesn't allow brake torquing (building boost or engine rpm by using the brakes to load the engine).

ACCELERATION TO 60 MPH

CAR	track start	street start
Buick LeSabre (auto)	10.1	10.1
Dodge Stealth R/T Turbo	5.9	6.8
Mazda Protegé LX	8.8	9.7
M-B 300D 2.5 Turbo (auto)	11.2	12.2
Mercury Capri XR2	7.9	8.8
Nissan 300ZX Turbo (auto)	5.9	6.5
Porsche 928GT	5.2	5.5
Toyota Celica GT-S	9.5	10.3
Volvo 740 Turbo (auto)	7.2	7.5

Cars whose engines are peaky or suffer turbo lag, such as the Mazda Protegé LX and the Dodge Stealth R/T Turbo, lose about a second in the street start. Cars with lots of torque and a well-matched drivetrains, like the Porsche 928GT and the Buick LeSabre, don't suffer much at all.

This new test will never replace balls-out track testing as the ultimate measure of a car's acceleration. But as the 911 Turbo and the ZR-1 results show, it gives us a better idea about how easily that performance can be achieved in everyday driving. Look for it in future tests. —Csaba Csere

"One of the Ten Best in the World."

–Road & Track

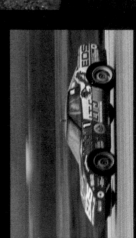

bumper's left corner and you'll notice that the turbocharger waste-gate outlet pipe is fitted with its own miniature catalytic converter.

The 911 Turbo's cabin is a mix of expensive Old World craftsmanship and just plain old. The soft leather on the four-spoke, air-bag-equipped wheel would do a very fine pair of gloves just swell. (You can option yourself to death as regards leather. See the sidebar story.) The pedals still hinge at the bottom, Beetle-style. Every piece of trim is impeccably battened down.

The dash remains the old 911 design: the gauge arrangement is still one of the best, with a tach the size of a salad plate located squarely in front of you. But the switchgear, much of it added over the years, is strewn about the instrument panel haphazardly. To Porsche's credit, it has managed to stuff a passenger-side air bag into the ancient dash layout.

Here's another voice:

Unlike the nasty north in winter, South Carolina is all sunshine, so Deputy Slide Rule Schroeder cannot tolerate one more minute behind the wheel of a Corvette ZR-1 coated with Kosher-size salt chunks and grease globules from Michigan and Ohio. We pull into Bob's Car Wash in Columbia. Bob's is crowded. Just before our turn on the roller track, we measure the Vette's left-rear tire to be sure it will fit. It's 12.75 inches wide; the track of the car wash is a tenth of an inch wider. Could be close. Ten feet into the wash, the Vette gets stuck, and refuses to move forward into its bath. Schroeder must back it out over the rollers, holding up a restless

Vital Statistics

		price, base/as tested	engine	SAE net power/torque	transmission/ gear ratios: 1/ maximum test speed, mph/ axle ratio:1	curb weight, lb	weight distribution % F/R
	CHEVROLET CORVETTE ZR-1	$64,138/$68,135	DOHC 32-valve V-8, 350 cu in (5727cc), aluminum block and heads, GM engine-control system with port fuel injection	375 bhp @ 5800 rpm/ 370 lb-ft @ 4800 rpm	6-speed/ 2.68, 1.80, 1.29, 1.00, 0.75, 0.50/ 56, 83, 114, 150, 171, 149/ 3.45	3519	52.4/47
	PORSCHE 911 TURBO	$95,000/$105,191	turbocharged and intercooled SOHC flat 6, 201 cu in (3299cc), aluminum block and heads, Bosch K-Jetronic fuel injection	315 bhp @ 5750 rpm/ 332 lb-ft @ 4500 rpm	5-speed/ 3.15, 1.79, 1.27, 0.97, 0.76/ 44, 77, 109, 143, 166/ 3.44	3270	38.7/61

C/D Test Results

		acceleration, sec									
		0–30 mph	0–60 mph	0–100 mph	0–130 mph	0–150 mph	1/4-mile	top gear, 30–50 mph	top gear, 50–70 mph	top speed, mph	braking 70–0 mph
	CHEVROLET CORVETTE ZR-1	2.1	4.9	11.2	20.0	35.5	13.2 @ 108 mph	13.1	13.2	171	155
	PORSCHE 911 TURBO	1.7	4.4	10.7	20.0	38.4	12.9 @ 108 mph	12.0	10.0	166	167

48

crowd. Luckily, they're too amused that our fancy car will have to be hand-washed in Bob's driveway to be angry. We don't get the Glow Wax, but we don't have to pay, either. Thanks, Bob. —Phil Berg

The view out of the 911 is very un–sports car. You sit bolt upright in the deeply winged seats, and you crank the seatback up even further in order to make the long reach to the steering wheel. The 911 is noticeably taller than the Vette, five inches in fact. The front window is nearly vertical, and the hood is short—this is a rear-engined car, remember—so the view out is superb. Your field of vision could not be better even if you sat on the hood.

Even if Porsche had put a '51 Studebaker body over this chassis, you'd know what was underneath by the time you got a mile down the road. Everything your five senses register harks back through 25 years of Porsche 911 history. The engine, for instance, emits the same hard-edged thrum Porsche flat sixes have always made. And why not? It's a mildly reworked version of the previous model's single-turbo 3.3-liter powerplant. Even its Jekyll-and-Hyde personality is there, though more subtle than before. At low revs the big turbocharger is barely ticking over, and the engine feels like it has its feet up on the desk; you have time to recite the first stanza of *Beowulf* before the boost comes up. But above three grand, the 911 Turbo is on a caffeine high. Put your foot down and hold on: the speedo needle blurs past 60 mph in

4.4 seconds and you're through the quarter-mile in 12.9 seconds at 108 mph.

The Turbo's parentage really comes into focus when you press hard. Drive it to 85 percent of its cornering potential and it's sweet and sophisticated. It reacts confidently. The steering is sensitive and accurate, with just the right weighting. And no 911 Turbo was ever so stable in a straight line at speeds above the century mark.

But turn it loose on a back road looking for that last fifteen percent and the Turbo acts up in much the manner of the previous version. It is a double handful in the corners, pitching and twitching like it longs to visit that ditch—a disobedient, thrusting animal trying to break its leash, or, if it doesn't get its way, its own neck. On the racetrack, the Turbo's mean streak made us conservative and kept it from getting within two seconds a lap of the ZR-1.

But it sure sounded good:

What kind of noise does $170,000 buy? The right kind, if you're watching these cars from the finish line at the half-mile front straightaway of Roebling Road. Even under full throttle, the 911 Turbo approaches with an uncanny, freight-train-like silence. But as it passes, the hint of rushing wind transforms into an explosion of guttural ripping.

On the other hand, the 911 is a gentleman compared with the ZR-1, which, when flat out, seems like a car gone mad. Rounding the final curve in third gear, it cries out, clearly audible and urgent, its rising wail becoming almost frightening as it approaches and blasts past at

more than 120 mph. A straining LT-5 is a great conversation stopper. —Don Schroeder

When the stunt driving is through, you'll find that the 911 is a decent, though not exceptional, long-distance companion. The ride is stiff. The engine is reasonably subdued, but road noise rolls through the cabin, and the rigid body registers each tar strip with a loud *pong!* worthy of a timpani drum. For a car bearing this price burden, the 911 ought to be equipped with a sound system better matched to its difficult acoustics; the one in our car sounded muddy when we turned it up enough to counter the rumble of the road.

But doubtlessly, this is one hell of a car. Masculine, powerful, threatening, beautiful, and fast. German. Unfortunately, it comes with one hell of a price tag. That, more than anything else, is what relegated it to a close second-place finish.

Chevrolet Corvette ZR-1 First Place

The ZR-1 triumphed over the 911 Turbo for one simple reason: it goes fast better. A ZR-1 in full stride is a highly talented athlete. It's always on its toes. Its moves are intuitive. Its speed is sudden and explosive. If you lust after a ZR-1 for any other reason than the thrill it delivers when you hammer it, perhaps you will be disappointed.

Unlike the Porsche, the Vette is not a car for preening. For one thing, there's nothing about it that's exclusive—at least

dimensions, in				fuel tank, gal	suspension		brakes, F/R	tires
wheel-base	length	width	height		front	rear		
96.2	178.5	73.2	46.7	20.0	ind, unequal-length control arms, transverse plastic leaf spring, 3-position cockpit-adjustable electronically controlled shock absorbers, anti-roll bar	ind; fixed-length half-shaft, 2 lateral links and 2 trailing links per side; transverse plastic leaf spring; 3-position cockpit-adjustable electronically controlled shock absorbers; anti-roll bar	vented disc/ vented disc; anti-lock control	Goodyear Eagle ZR40; F: P275/40ZR-17, R: P315/35ZR-17
89.5	168.3	69.9	51.6	20.3	ind, strut located by a control arm, coil springs, anti-roll bar	ind, semi-trailing arm, coil springs, anti-roll bar	vented disc/ vented disc; anti-lock control	Bridgestone Expedia S-01; F: 205/50ZR-17, R: 255/40ZR-17

roadholding, 300-ft skidpad, g	maneuverability, 1000-ft slalom, mph	interior sound level, dBA				fuel economy, mpg			racecourse, min:sec
		idle	full throttle	70-mph cruising	70-mph coasting	EPA city	EPA hwy	C/D observed	
0.87	68.0	57	89	78	77	16	25	17	1:27.3
0.91	66.3	63	82	77	76	13	21	16	1:29.8

49

not visibly. This year, every Corvette shares the ZR-1's concave tail, and all Vettes wear the same new nosepiece. Only a small ZR-1 badge and a few subtle body parts set it off. We're convinced that our ZR-1 got all the attention it did because it was always in the company of the strutting Porsche.

The ZR-1 doesn't exhibit the fit-and-finish quality one is entitled to expect in a $64,000 car. The interior fit seems half-hearted, and some of the inside plastic has a decidedly low-ball look. Some items as the hard-to-read gauges and the fluttery hood failed to meet the quality expectations engendered by the wonderful powertrain. Even the transmission on our car rattled ominously at idle, and it's a sound we've heard before from other Corvettes.

Time out for a sobering observation:

Speed enforcement appears to be the growth industry of the South. We're subjected to more microwave interrogations in one day than we deal with in a month up North. Now we're getting zapped again. What's with these guys? We've been on the road only an hour, and already we've seen seven patrol cars. That's one every nine miles.

The troopers are cagey, too. An ice-blue Thunderbird—unmarked, of course—has one poor sucker pulled over. A black T-Bird running radar passes us a half-mile down the road. We see a silver Mustang and a black-and-white Taurus going the other way on South Carolina I-385. You'll never pick them out in your mirror.

The most depressing part about this constant police omnipresence is that it works. Everyone on the road is cowed. No one dares venture more than five over the limit. Not even us.

—Rich Ceppos

Put the ZR-1 into motion and you'll forget all about things like upholstery and shaky hood panels. You sit down low, in a thick-walled cocoon, but the initial feeling of isolation melts away in moments. The deeply pocketed seats are excellent, and the shifter, wheel, and pedals are positioned perfectly.

The first surprise is the ZR-1's ride: it can do a fair impression of a sedan, if you ask that of it. The key is the standard-equipment electronically controlled shock absorbers, which offer three damping programs, ranging from plush to racer-stiff. (We found the middle setting best for all-around use.) This roughneck indeed has table manners.

Fortunately, not too many manners. The big V-8 makes sure of that. Lots of displacement—5.7 liters in all—breathing through 32 valves makes for instant

JEFFREY DWORIN

Why Isn't This Cow Smiling?

• Why? Because it's udderly confused and amazed at the number of custom leather-covered items offered as options in the 911 Turbo. Playing big spender with the order form will add $12,742 to the Turbo's already bloated sticker. You can choose from 42 special-order leather items in the Turbo that range from extra-soft leather seats to, well, see for yourself:

Item:	Suggested Retail
Extra-soft leather seats	$360
Leather instrument housing	1353
Leather instrument trim rings	398
Leather gearbox tunnel	181
Leather covered tray	161
Leather door-lock knob and bezel	349
Leather ignition lock plate	66
Leather ignition key	158
Leather shift knob	241
Leather control knobs on dash	648
Leather glove-box knob	91
Leather turn-signal lever	246
Leather power window switches	294
Leather inside door opener	174
Leather dash fresh-air vents	646
Leather fresh-air vents	312
Leather parking-brake lever	236
Leather seatback lock and housing	402
Leather radio-speaker grilles	418
Leather seat hinges	315
Leather front-seat backrest lock	448
Leather fresh-air vent covers	18
Leather control-panel cover	269
Leather heater switches	85
Leather seat-adjuster switches	330
Leather seat-adjuster switches	305
Leather fuel-tank pull-knob flap	55
Leather outside-mirror control knob	32
Leather safety-belt covers	100
Leather front safety-belt rosettes	136
Leather rear safety-belt housings	531
Leather rear-wiper switches	166
Leather light switch	83
Leather wiper instrument light knob	96
Leather door-lock pin rosettes	42
Leather warning-buzzer rosette	50
Leather covered caps	15
Leather entrance-panel cover	241
Leather sunvisor	631
Leather welting	922
Leather piping	108
Leather roofliner	1030

lunge whenever your right foot twitches. Our test car was slightly slower than other ZR-1s we've driven, but it still managed a 0-to-60 pass in 4.9 seconds and a quarter-mile blast of 13.2 seconds at 108 mph. And the sounds—great booming, thrashing howling blasts—stand your wrist hair on end.

Meanwhile, out on the highway:

The 911 Turbo and the ZR-1 are the sharks of the Interstates. Our test cars attract these pilot fish, these remoras, which cling to our flanks. Two of these tailgaters make dangerous moves just to keep close on northbound I-75. A Georgia-plated Passat latches onto the back of the ZR-1 and stays there from Tennessee to Cincinnati. When we pull off the freeway for fuel, to make the exit behind us the Passat cuts off a hapless Mazda pickup. We leave him at the pumps,

but fifteen minutes of VW-flogging returns him to our draft.

Of special note is a Suzuki Swift from South Carolina containing two girls and an infant that keeps up with our 85-mph pace. A Pontiac 2000 and a Mercedes 300CE, both from Ohio, trade tailgating spots with the Suzuki, making our convoy a conspicuous train of five cars. (Hey, let's all room together next semester!) It makes no difference if we slow to a crawl, none of our pilot fish will pass the sharks. Even a quick blast to 140 mph fails to shake them permanently; our unwelcome followers drone along determinedly until they catch up.

A gunmetal-gray Legend would be much easier—and safer—to drive across the country.
—Phil Berg

The Vette's behavior on twisting two-lane roads is every bit as exciting as what

it does in a straight line. It goes where you aim it. Period. No feints, lurches, or false moves. It hangs on as if it had giant asphalt-piercing spikes in its tires. The Corvette ZR-1 is the equivalent Isiah Thomas: both do the seemingly impossible moves and somehow make it look easy.

Ease off to catch your breath and it's apparent that the Vette is a thoroughly docile creature around town. The controls are light and precise, and every amenity except heated seats is on duty to serve you. You could commute to work in this car.

But when you slow down and mingle with the ordinaries, it becomes for all the world just another Corvette. You have to love this car for the wild animal within, and nothing more. ●

	engine	transmission	brakes	handling	ride	comfort	ergonomics	fit and finish	value	audacity	fun to drive	OVERALL RATING
CHEVROLET CORVETTE ZR-1	9	7	9	9	7	7	8	5	7	8	9	89
PORSCHE 911 TURBO	8	7	10	8	7	7	7	10	5	9	9	86

Three editors rated the vehicles in each of twelve categories; the scores presented are averages. A 1-to-10 scale (10 being best) was used for all categories except the Overall Rating, where a 1-to-100 scale was used. The Overall Rating for each vehicle was assigned independently; it is not a summation of the vehicle's points in the other categories.

Editors' Ratings

WE WROTE THE BOOK ON V8 PERFORMANCE. WAIT TILL YOU GET YOUR HANDS ON THE SEQUEL.

THE 300-HP ADVANCED TRACTION CONTROL CHEVROLET CORVETTE LT1

The new 5.7 Liter LT1 V8 is the most technically advanced small block in Chevy history. And only one machine has it: The new 1992 Corvette. The LT1 engine generates seamless, effortless power. The kind that makes an enthusiast's mouth water. And the Corvette also features Acceleration Slip Regulation (ASR), a highly sophisticated traction control system that regulates the application of power to the rear wheels, providing optimum grip in all traction conditions. Test drive the 1992 Corvette LT1. Cover to cover, it's the best 'Vette yet.

THE HEARTBEAT OF AMERICA IS WINNING.

Chevrolet Corvette

If, as they say, God is in the details, then this is the first holy Corvette.

BY CSABA CSERE

Chevrolet has presented new Corvettes that have stimulated our cranial synapses with exotic new technology, elevated our pulses with bump-and-grind styling, and sent our adrenal glands into overload with tire-scorching performance, but this new 1997 model is the first Corvette that presses all of our livable and useful buttons with its relentless attention to detail and meticulous engineering.

Dubbed the C5 because it is the fifth-generation Corvette, the new model uses a structure that is four times as stiff as the C4 chassis. Its natural frequency measures 23 hertz, close to the Mercedes E320's and the Oldsmobile Aurora's, which are among the stiffest cars in the world. Furthermore, this stiffness only drops to 21 hertz when the roof panel is removed.

The stiffer structure does much to reduce the squeaks and rattles that have always plagued Corvettes, but chief engineer Dave Hill didn't stop there. From day one, he assigned an engineer to do nothing but optimize the design and assembly of every part to eliminate unwanted noise. Among the items eliminated were 34 percent of the total number of parts in the C4. By using fewer, larger parts, the C5 is inherently more solid.

Despite the reduction in the number of parts, the C5 has grown: slightly on the outside, substantially inside. In addition to offering more room for large people, a lower sill and a taller roofline make it easier to enter and exit. The pop-out roof panel is now attached with three hand levers rather than four bolts and a ratchet wrench. Meanwhile, luggage space has doubled to 25 cubic feet, more than a Saab 900's.

Completely new suspension geometry at both ends has greatly reduced the C4's tendency to be pummeled by potholes, deflected by crowned roads, and upset by truck grooves on the road. The new model seems glued to the road, without transmitting all surface imperfections to its occupants.

As valuable as these improvements are, however, they would be worthless had they been achieved at the expense of performance. We're happy to report that in the pursuit of their kinder and gentler priorities, Dave Hill and his team have not forgotten that speed is central to the Corvette experience.

Despite a softer launch at Atlanta Dragway than we normally achieve at our sticky test track in Michigan, the preproduction 1997 Corvette hit 60 mph in 4.9 seconds and 100 mph in 11.4 seconds and swallowed up the quarter-mile in 13.4 seconds at 108 mph.

We were only able to reach 130 mph within the short confines of the drag strip, and that figure came up in 20.5 seconds, but Chevrolet claims a top speed of 172 mph. Jim Ingle, a Corvette development engineer and known straight shooter, assured us that he's seen 175 mph at the 7.5-mile Transportation Research Center's oval in Ohio.

The quickest LT1-engined C4 we've ever tested needed 13.6 seconds at 104 mph to cover the quarter. The fastest one topped out at 161 mph. Even the hotted-up LT4-engined car we tested last year

could only run 13.7 at 104 and top out at 168. In fact, we've tested relatively slow ZR-1s that could barely keep up with the new C5. Despite its newfound comfort and practicality, the C5 is, without question, one of the fastest Corvettes ever.

This combination of speed, utility, and solidity is clothed in completely new body-work—still fiberglass, of course—that is both sleek and reminiscent of past Corvettes. To many eyes, however, there are a few styling genes from the Mazda RX-7 and Pontiac Firebird evident in its low, rounded, twin-nostriled front end.

In profile, the C5 is low in front and a little heavy in the rump, as if it were mid-engined. Practically speaking, the low nose enhances forward visibility and the high tail reduces drag and increases lug-gage space, but the look takes a bit of get-ting used to.

At the rear, this bodywork terminates

in a sharp crease that seems incongruous with the rounded contours elsewhere. The necessarily tall rear fascia is nicely broken up by four oval taillights near the top and an array of slots near the bottom. Unfor-tunately, the four flat-black exhaust tips virtually disappear when viewed from a distance. A few square inches of polished stainless steel would find a good home here.

Despite these nits, we don't dislike the look of the C5. It just doesn't knock our socks off. But pretty is as pretty does, and the new body boasts an excellent drag coefficient of 0.29—a useful improvement over the C4's 0.34 figure.

Some of this benefit is offset by the greater frontal area, a result of the C5's being 1.4 inches taller and 2.9 inches wider than the C4 (it's almost as wide as the dis-continued ZR-1). Allowing for this increase, the C5 still produces about 8.5

percent less aerodynamic drag than its pre-decessor. Lift—and the resulting high-speed instability that it can provoke—was never a problem with the C4, but insiders report that the C5 body is about 30 percent improved by that measure as well.

This coachwork covers a completely redesigned chassis that was conceived to finally give the Corvette the solid founda-tion it needed to shed its reputation for a jittery ride and low-quality assembly. Greater interior space, easier entry and exit, and a more solid mounting for the suspension pieces were also high on the new chassis agenda.

A folded-steel backbone—roughly 12 inches high, 9 inches wide, and 4 feet long—forms the heart of this frame. With a bottom plate attached by 36 bolts turning it into an enclosed tube, this structure pro-vides immense torsional rigidity.

The sheetmetal flares out at each end

to tie into the C5's second major structural element: a pair of hydroformed rectangular-section steel rails that run the full length of the car, just inside the front and rear wheels and kicking out to form the door sills next to the passenger compartment.

These galvanized-steel elements begin as six-inch-diameter tubes. They are first roughly bent to shape and then inserted into a set of dies. The tubes are then filled with water at a pressure of 5000 psi, which forces them into their four-by-six-inch rectangular configuration. They provide much of the C5's bending stiffness.

A steel roll-bar structure is welded to the rear intersection of these frame rails and the backbone frame. At the front intersection, two rectangular steel tubes jut upward to provide mounting points for the aluminum windshield structure.

Featherweight pieces are everywhere

on the frame. The steering column is supported by a magnesium casting. The removable roof panel also uses magnesium for its frame. The floor boards are a composite of fiberglass and balsa wood. No one can accuse Hill and his team of taking shortcuts in the design of this chassis.

One might, however, come to a different conclusion after a first glance at the new LS1 engine, which superficially appears to be another rehash of the 31-year-old small-block V-8. But the LS1, which we thoroughly discussed in Technical Highlights last October, shares nothing but its 4.4-inch bore spacing with its forebears.

The light-but-strong philosophy that pervades the C5 is evident in the LS1 engine as well. Its new aluminum block extends well below the crankshaft centerline and uses six bolts (four from the bottom and one from each side) to retain

each main-bearing cap. Each aluminum head attaches to this block with 10 bolts in a symmetrical four-bolt pattern around each bore, rather than the traditional five-bolt array. These bolts thread into the block down near the main-bearing web to minimize distortion of the cylinders bores when they are tightened.

These new heads employ equally spaced intake and exhaust ports rather than the traditional siamesed pattern. The lightweight plastic intake manifold takes advantage of this change with tuned intake runners and smooth interior surfaces.

The LS1 engine marks the debut of the Corvette's first drive-by-wire throttle. Instead of a mechanical linkage from the accelerator to open and close the throttle, the LS1 uses an electric motor. This motor is controlled by a computer that reads the position of a sensor at the accelerator pedal. It also incorporates the cruise-con-

■ Turn-Signal Stalk

The C5's windshield-wiper control stalk comes from the Oldsmobile Aurora, with one major modification: On an early test drive, former Chevrolet general manager Jim Perkins inadvertently pulled the stalk and activated the windshield washers. Knowing how Corvette owners would feel if they accidentally sprayed washer fluid on a car they had spent hours polishing, he mandated that the washer switch be moved to a button on the end of the stalk.

trol system and communicates with the engine-management computer and the traction-control system to restrict engine output when needed. By combining all these functions, it is actually simpler and lighter than the conventional setup.

In contrast to this innovation, you might be surprised to see that the LS1 engine retains the traditional pushrod, two-valve design. But lightweight valves, extensive use of roller bearings, and optimized valvetrain geometry have reduced friction while maintaining a lofty redline of 6000 rpm.

Moreover, the LS1 is distantly related to an upcoming new truck V-8, which will be built in huge volumes. That genealogy

may well have dictated the pushrod setup as well as the tight bore spacing that forces the LS1 engine to have a smaller bore and longer stroke than the old V-8.

But with 345 horsepower and 350 pound-feet of torque, a light 532-pound weight, compact dimensions, and projected EPA fuel-economy figures of 18 city and 28 highway with a manual trans-

mission, it's hard to fault Chevy's design decisions.

This engine feeds its output to the rear wheels via an all-new driveline that positions the transmission in the tail. A torque tube that is five inches in diameter and four feet long connects the engine rigidly to the new rear-mounted transaxle. The entire assembly attaches to the chassis via a

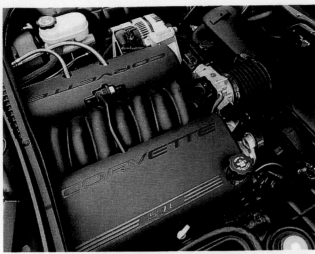

■ Foreign-Language Warnings
In preparation for foreign sales, the messages on the driver's-information center can be displayed in English, French, Spanish, or German, at the driver's option.

hydraulic mount underneath the transaxle and a motor mount on either side of the engine block.

With a manual transmission, the hydraulically operated clutch is bolted to the engine's flywheel. The clutch in turn twists an aluminum-and-ceramic-matrix driveshaft. The gearbox is a variation of the Borg-Warner T56 used in the Chevrolet Camaro and Dodge Viper. For use in the C5, its guts are reinforced with triple cone synchronizers in the lower gears and stuffed into a new case that bolts to a Getrag limited-slip differential.

If you're being picky, this isn't really a transaxle, since the transmission and the differential each have their own discrete cases and do not share lubricants, but other than costing a few pounds and maybe an inch in length, that's not a disadvantage.

If you specify an automatic, the arrangement is much the same except that the torque converter is mounted in the rear with the transmission, a Hydra-Matic 4L60-E, which is a repackaged version of the C4's four-speed automatic.

By moving the transmission from the front to the rear, Hill and his engineers created more space for wider footwells—six inches wider on the passenger side. Moving the transmission aft also helped restore the weight distribution to nearly even—it was 51.4/48.6 on our test sample—after such measures as pulling the rear wheels back, moving the gas tank forward, and eliminating the spare tire had increased the front weight bias.

The keen reader will have noticed the implications of the hydraulic mounting of this differential. Since 1963, when Corvettes first received independent rear suspensions, their differentials were always solidly mounted because the half-shafts formed the upper suspension links. On the C5, this is no longer so.

Instead, the rear suspension consists of unequal-length aluminum upper and lower control arms with a rear-mounted toe-control link. The lower control arms mount to a cast-aluminum subframe that is bolted solidly to the chassis. The upper control arms attach to the hydroformed side rails. The half-shafts are now a splined design to accommodate the length variations imposed by suspension movement. A transverse plastic leaf spring is the only element even vaguely recognizable from the C4.

The suspension geometry was conceived to provide minimal track and toe changes as the wheels move up and down. The toe-control link is critical to achieving this, especially since the bushings allow the wheels to move rearward slightly to help absorb small, sharp bumps.

In front, the design philosophy is similar, with unequal-length control arms and a transverse plastic leaf spring mounted to another large cast-aluminum subframe. In place of the toe-control link, you'll find GM's Magnasteer II setup.

Magnasteer II is a refinement of the rotary electromagnetic variable-assist power-steering system that made its debut on the Aurora. The computer that controls this electromagnet now looks at speed and lateral acceleration to provide a more stable, progressive feel at the steering-wheel rim.

The base suspension has gas-charged, single-tube shock absorbers all around. Optional is the F45 variable-damping system that provides three cockpit settings. Each setting corresponds to a different program that selects from an infinite variety of damping curves based on wheel travel, steering-wheel angle, and calculated lateral acceleration. Called Selective Real Time Damping, the system can change the shock settings as often as 100 times *per second*.

Finally, for committed performance enthusiasts, there's the Z51 option that comes with larger (1.8- versus 1.4-inch diameter) gas-charged shocks with a single setting (stiffer than any of the F45 offerings), along with stiffer springs and larger anti-roll bars.

As on the C4, there are vented disc brakes and aluminum calipers at each corner. Although the front rotors are slightly smaller in diameter than previously, they are substantially thicker, as are the rears. Furthermore, the two openings in the C5's front fascia feed cooling air via four-inch ducts to the front brakes. Anti-lock control is provided by a Bosch ABS V system that is integrated with the standard traction-control system.

All this chassis hardware communicates with the pavement via Goodyear Eagle F1 GS EMT tires—P245/45ZR-17 in front and P275/40ZR-18 in the rear. You will notice that for the first time in Corvette history the rear tire is larger in diameter than the front, for appearance and because the resulting longer contact patch provides some stability benefits.

You might also notice that both tires are one size *narrower* than the C4's, although we were told that the new car achieves 0.92 g on the skidpad compared with 0.89 for the old one. With sufficient grip, the narrower tires provide better steering feel and greater tolerance of imperfect pavement.

Sliding behind the wheel of the

■ Flat Bottom

It's easy to forget that the underside of a car is aerodynamically as important as the top side. The Corvette engineers didn't, as you can see by examining the C5's nearly flat bottom. By carefully shaping these hidden parts and tucking the exhaust system into the bottom of the central tunnel, they made sure air would be almost as happy flowing under the car as it is over it.

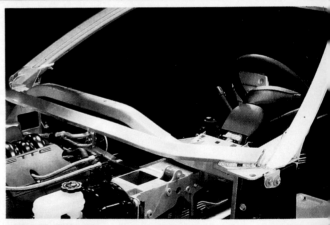

■ Windshield Structure

The framework that forms the windshield surround, dashboard mounting, and front rollover structure is fabricated from welded aluminum extrusions and castings for light weight, which is particularly beneficial so high in the car.

■ Magnesium Steering Column

A large, comprehensively ribbed-and-braced magnesium casting provides a light yet rock-solid mounting for the steering column and the pedal assembly.

■ Front Chassis Subframe

A large, well-braced aluminum subframe spans the underside of the C5 at each end. The front subframe, shown here, provides a rigid mounting for the suspension's lower controls arms and anti-roll bar, as well as the steering rack.

C5 certainly demands less human origami than before, and the greater view out from the cockpit makes the C5 feel more like an Acura NSX than the C4 with its somewhat buried perspective.

Ergonomically, the C5 is hard to fault. The wider footwells provide room for a perfectly positioned dead pedal. The wipers are controlled by a stalk sprouting from the *right* of the steering column. The steering column itself is adjustable for angle, although not reach, and comes with a fat, grippy rim and spokes well positioned for hands at the three- and nine-o'clock positions. The shift knob is no more than a hand's breadth away from the rim. The ignition switch is on the dash rather than the steering column.

And to our immense relief, the C5 has a full set of proper, round, white-on-black instruments that are neither a weak imitation of an arcade game nor afflicted with any needles that fall as the temperature rises.

Not that there's a total absence of razzle-dazzle. When you fire up the C5, the needles on all the instruments flick full scale and back, and a driver-information center uses an alphanumeric display to communicate a wide variety of information, including the individual pressure in each of the C5's four tires (good to know because an inattentive driver might not realize when the run-flat tires are underinflated).

As you accumulate miles in the C5, the claims about the improved rigidity become fully credible. Bumps produce single, muted thumps with no quivers, no rattles, and no aftershocks. There's also no sign of the C4's fondness for continuous tiny vertical shakes that made us feel as if we were sitting on the end of a springy diving board. Finally, the C4 suspension's tendency to turn vertical bumps into small lateral vibrations—occasionally even on a straight road—is completely absent.

The preproduction examples we drove did, however, exhibit more driveline noise than we expected. In one, the engine buzzed lightly between 3000 and 5000 rpm. In another, there was some rattling in first gear. With the C5's sophisticated driveline isolation, we hope

these vibrations will be exorcised before cars arrive at dealerships.

When you start pushing the C5 hard on a winding road, the body moves up and down as needed to absorb the bumps and grinds of the pavement, but the four tires

■ Alternator Bracket
Is this the beefiest alternator mounting bracket you've ever seen? Realizing that a smooth engine is meaningless if the accessories vibrate, Chevrolet engineers mounted all the LS1's auxiliary components very rigidly. The air-conditioning compressor doesn't even use brackets–it bolts directly to the block.

■ Suspension Mounts
The C5's front upper control arm pivots on bushings mounted solidly to the hydroformed outer rail. On the previous-model Corvette, the control arm attached to a pivot rod that hung from the front structure.

■ Rear Suspension, Rear View
On the C4, the rear shock absorbers bolted to the upper trailing link that was attached to the suspension using soft bushings. On the C5, the shocks attach to the lower control arm near the upright. As a result, small wheel movements that were lost in the bushings before reaching the shock absorbers on the C4 are fully damped on the C5.

feel as if they're magnetically attached to the pavement.

In cars equipped with the adjustable F45 suspension, this supple character prevails in all three settings, although the level of ride control increases progressively as you dial the switch from "tour" to "sport" to "performance." But even the tautest setting is far less harsh than it was on, say, the 1995 FX3-equipped models.

Such a stable platform encourages hard charging. The precise and progressive control responses will help all C5 drivers imitate Alain Prost. The lengthy shift linkage communing with the rear-mounted transaxle feels precise and accurate. The stopping power of the strong brakes varies linearly with the pressure of your foot on the cast-aluminum brake pedal. Furthermore, there's a nice gradual onset of braking when your foot first starts pressing the pedal, making you look smooth even when you stab the brakes to cope with an over-the-rise surprise.

The steering proves equally friendly, although at first we felt that the effort was a little too heavy. But as we proceeded to attack the winding and hilly back roads of Kentucky, the steering became completely transparent. There seemed to be a seamless connection between the driver's brain and the C5's front tires without the need for any conscious thought. You can eat up pavement very quickly and easily in this car without ever breaking a sweat or sliding a tire. However, we were given the opportunity to do both at Road Atlanta racetrack. We were critically interested in the C5's behavior at the limit, because the C4 was particularly forgiving when driven flat out. Despite its high limits, you could lean hard on it, safe in the belief that it would break away gradually and keep its tail in line.

We soon developed the same confidence in the C5, although with the new car's higher grip, it

■ Tunnel Cutaway
This cutaway shows that, in addition to housing the torque tube, the C5's structural backbone also provides a conduit for brake and fuel lines, the shift linkage, the wiring harness, and on the other side, the parking-brake cable. A flat panel closes off these components in the upper two-thirds of the tunnel, providing room for the exhaust system underneath.

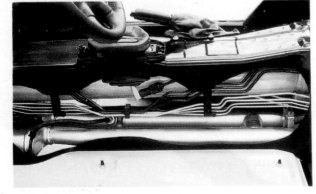

The C5 vs. the Fastest and Slowest Corvettes We've Tested

	C1 (1953–62)*		C2 (1963–67)		C3 (1968–82)		C4 (1984–96)		C5
	best	worst	best	worst	best	worst	best	worst	
model	1957	1956	1966	1965	1969	1975	1990 ZR-1	1984	1997
tested	Jun '57	May '56	Nov '65	Jan '65	Sep '69	May '75	Jun '89	Oct '83	Feb '97
power, bhp	283 gross	225 gross	425 gross	350 gross	435 gross	165 net	385 net	205 net	345 net
displacement, cubic inches	283	265	427	327	427	350	349	350	346
curb weight, pounds	2840	2980	3450	3180	3450	3690	3440	3237	3260
price as tested	$3890	$3761	$5666	$5276	$6573	$8352	$51,500	$24,376	$41,000 (est)
0–60 mph, seconds	6.6	7.5	5.4	6.2	5.3	7.7	4.5	6.7	4.9
standing 1/4-mile, seconds	14.2 @ 93 mph	15.9 @ 91 mph	12.8 @ 112 mph	14.9 @ 94 mph	13.8 @ 107 mph	16.1 @ 87 mph	12.8 @ 111 mph	15.1 @ 91 mph	13.4 @ 108 mph
top speed, mph	125	120	153 (est)	130 (est)	138 (est)	129	175	142	172 (est)

*Car and Driver's predecessor, Sports Cars Illustrated, was born in 1956, so no six-cylinder Corvette test data are included.

definitely takes more speed before it slides. Through the 70-to-90-mph esses at Road Atlanta, the C5 only gradually relinquishes its grip on the asphalt. Unlike the C4, the new model does slide first at the tail, but after oozing out only a few degrees, it stabilizes in a slight drift. Easing off the throttle a tiny amount brings the car right back into line.

In slower turns, such as the right-angle, second-gear corner leading onto the back straight, you can get the tail out big time if you are even slightly overaggressive with the throttle—with the traction control turned off, of course. Not even the Dodge Viper GTS demands as much respect in similar turns.

As it turns out, Corvette engineers plan a few changes prior to production to minimize this behavior. A five-percent-stiffer front spring will increase understeer slightly, and a change in the rear-tire com-

pound is expected to increase cornering grip when the power is hard on.

Those who perennially hope for a smaller Corvette will be disappointed, but there's no question that the C5 uses its bulk well. Moreover, it is not overweight for its size or performance. The now-defunct Nissan 300ZX Turbo weighed 300 pounds more than this new C5, and the Toyota Supra Turbo and the Mitsubishi 3000GT VR4 are heavier than it as well. Only the far smaller Porsche 911 undercuts the C5's weight—and then by less than 200 pounds.

Which brings us to another Corvette tradition that the C5 upholds: exotic-car

performance at a moderate price. The least expensive production car we've tested that can outperform the C5 in the quarter-mile is the Dodge Viper RT/10, which costs $65,260. Although final C5 pricing has not yet been announced, Chevrolet plans to price it not much higher than the C4's $38,000 base price.

Corvettes, of course, have always delivered tremendous performance for the buck. But purists have tended to dismiss this value by reciting the litany of quality and refinement shortcomings that accompanied it. With the C5, that list is suddenly very short indeed. ●

C/D TEST RESULTS

ACCELERATION
	Seconds
Zero to 30 mph	2.1
40 mph	2.9
50 mph	3.8
60 mph	4.9
70 mph	6.1
80 mph	7.8
90 mph	9.5
100 mph	11.4
110 mph	14.0
120 mph	16.8
130 mph	20.5
Street start, 5–60 mph	5.5
Top-gear passing time, 30–50 mph	11.6
50–70 mph	11.7
Standing 1/4-mile	13.4 sec @ 108 mph
Top speed (estimated)	172 mph

BRAKING
70–0 mph @ impending lockup ....163 ft
Fade ....**none** light moderate heavy

PROJECTED FUEL ECONOMY
EPA city driving ....**18 mpg**
EPA highway driving ....**28 mpg**
C/D observed fuel economy ....**18 mpg**

INTERIOR SOUND LEVEL
Idle ....56 dBA
Full-throttle acceleration ....84 dBA
70-mph cruising ....73 dBA
70-mph coasting ....72 dBA

CHEVROLET CORVETTE
Vehicle type: front-engine, rear-wheel-drive, 2-passenger, 2-door targa

Estimated price as tested: $41,000 (estimated base price: $39,000)

Options on test car: dual-zone A/C, CD changer, sport seats, fog lamps

Major standard accessories: power steering, windows, driver's seat, and locks, A/C, cruise control, tilting steering wheel, rear defroster

Sound system: Delco AM/FM-stereo radio/CD changer, 4 speakers

ENGINE
Type ....V-8, aluminum block and heads
Bore x stroke ....3.90 x 3.62 in, 99.0 x 92.0mm
Displacement ....346 cu in, 5665cc
Compression ratio 10.0:1
Engine-control system ....GM with port fuel injection
Emissions controls ....3-way catalytic converter, feedback air-fuel-ratio control, auxiliary air pump
Valve gear ....pushrods, 2 valves per cylinder, hydraulic lifters
Power (SAE net) ....345 bhp @ 5600 rpm
Torque (SAE net) ....350 lb-ft @ 4400 rpm
Redline ....6000 rpm

DRIVETRAIN
Transmission ....6-speed manual
Final-drive ratio ....3.42:1, limited slip
Gear	Ratio	Mph/1000 rpm	Max. speed in gears
I	2.66	8.4	50 mph (6000 rpm)
II	1.78	12.6	75 mph (6000 rpm)
III	1.30	17.2	103 mph (6000 rpm)
IV	1.00	22.4	134 mph (6000 rpm)
V	0.74	30.2	172 mph (5700 rpm)
VI	0.50	44.8	172 mph (3850 rpm)

DIMENSIONS AND CAPACITIES
Wheelbase ....104.5 in
Track, F/R ....62.0/62.1 in
Length ....179.7 in
Width ....73.6 in

Height ....47.7 in
Ground clearance ....3.7 in
Curb weight ....3260 lb
Weight distribution, F/R 51.5/48.5%
Fuel capacity ....19.1 gal
Oil capacity ....6.5 qt
Water capacity ....11.4 qt

CHASSIS/BODY
Type ....full-length frame integral with body
Body material ....fiberglass-reinforced plastic

INTERIOR
SAE volume, front seat ....52 cu ft
luggage space ....25 cu ft
Front seats ....bucket
Seat adjustments ....fore and aft, seatback angle, front height, rear height, lumbar support, upper side bolsters
Restraint systems, front ....manual 3-point belts, driver and passenger airbags
General comfort ....poor fair good **excellent**
Fore-and-aft support ....poor fair good **excellent**
Lateral support ....poor fair good **excellent**

SUSPENSION
F: ....ind, unequal-length control arms, transverse plastic leaf spring, anti-roll bar
R: ....ind, unequal-length control arms with a toe control link, transverse plastic leaf spring, anti-roll bar

STEERING
Type ....rack-and-pinion, power-assisted
Turns lock-to-lock 2.7
Turning circle curb-to-curb ....38.5 ft

BRAKES
F: ....12.8 x 1.3-in vented disc
R: ....12.0 x 1.0-in vented disc
Power assist ....vacuum with anti-lock control

WHEELS AND TIRES
Wheel size ....F: 8.5 x 17 in, R: 9.5 x 18 in
Wheel type ....cast aluminum
Tires ....Goodyear Eagle F1 GS EMT; F: P245/45ZR-17, R: P275/40ZR-18
Test inflation pressures, F/R ....30/30 psi

RAGTOP FACE-OFF: Boxster, M roadster, SLK320, TT Quattro

CAR AND DRIVER

AUGUST 2000 • CANADA $4.50   UK £2.50   US $3.50

Master of Speed!

385 hp Z06: Titanium mufflers, tenacious tires . . . The quickest Vette yet!

NEW: Acura MDX, BMW 330Ci and 330xi, Kia Rio.
TESTED: Audi Allroad, Dodge Neon R/T vs. Nissan Sentra SE.
PLUS: $482,000 tow truck, One Lap of America—again.

03915

0 272851 7

08

Chevrolet Corvette Z06

The latest in a long line of obscurely named Corvettes that go like stink.

BY CSABA CSERE

PHOTOGRAPHY BY AARON KILEY

Stumble upon a nest of Corvette aficionados, and you'll hear more obscure alphanumeric sequences than if you'd crept into a meeting of the U.S. Joint Chiefs of Staff. Back in 1963, codes such as L-88, ZR-1, M-22, and ZL-1 were created as internal designations for Corvette options, but they have since taken on deep and emotional meaning for the Corvette faithful.

For 2001, Chevrolet will rejuvenate a code from this hallowed list with the new model you see on these pages. Called the Z06, it represents a variant of the C5 Corvette enhanced with a comprehensive package of go-fast upgrades designed to make it the highest-performance production Corvette ever built. (In 1963, the Z06 code signified a racing package that included finned aluminum drum brakes, a beefed-up suspension, and a 36.5-gallon gas tank.)

The new Z06 starts with a more powul version of the Corvette's LS1 V-8 ngine. Designated the LS6, this engine mploys a redesigned intake manifold th smoother internal passages. Revised linder heads incorporate better-wing intake and exhaust ports, comstion chambers redesigned to reduce lve shrouding, and a higher compres-n ratio. New thin-walled cast-iron haust manifolds provide a smoother t for the combustion products.

To exploit the LS6's greater flow pacities at high rpm, the engineers ted a hotter camshaft with more valve erlap and greater valve lift, new rome-vanadium-steel valve springs, d stronger pistons cast from a more rable alloy. And to help air retreat m the underside of the flaying pistons, e LS6 has windows cast into the ernal crankcase walls.

These collective changes result in 385 rsepower at 6000 rpm, 385 pound-feet

of torque at 4800 rpm, and a redline of 6500 rpm—increases of 40 horsepower, 35 pound-feet, and 500 rpm, respectively, over the current LS1 engine. Incidentally, by fitting a few of the LS6 pieces to the LS1 V-8, that engine gets bumped 5 horsepower and 25 pound-feet for 2001.

The LS6 engine feeds its fortified output to the rear wheels via a beefed-up clutch (with lighter pedal effort), a larger-diameter driveshaft, and a revised six-speed manual transaxle. Called the M12, this new gearbox has shorter gearing (10 to 16 percent shorter, except for fourth gear, which is unchanged) to better exploit the LS6 engine's higher-revving power band.

Collectively, these powertrain changes vastly increase the Z06's available thrust and require major chassis revisions. As a result, the car gets a new FE4 suspension that includes revised

shock calibrations all-around, a stiffer rear transverse leaf spring, and stiffer anti-roll bars front and rear (larger diameter with thicker walls).

There are also larger tires and wheels, with the rim width going up one inch at all four corners to 9.5 inches in front and 10.5 inches in back. Wrapped around these enlarged wheels, which also sport a new 10-spoke design and are said to be very light, is a new Goodyear tire called the Eagle F1 SC. It was developed specifically for the Z06. The fronts are 265/40ZR-17s; the rears are 295/35ZR-18s—each 20 millimeters wider than the rubber on other Corvettes.

These Eagle F1 SCs dispense with the run-flat capability of the standard C5 tires. Consequently, they have more flexible sidewalls, which permit a half-degree more negative camber (0.75 degree instead of 0.25 degree) to keep the tread flatter during hard cornering.

41

THE VERDICT

Highs: Effortless power, fierce grip, excellent handling balance.

Lows: Busy ride on rough roads, modest interior finish for the price.

The Verdict: The Corvette's reputation for offering tremendous performance for the dollar enters the new millennium.

The Z06 model is distinguished by red cylinder-head covers, red brake calipers, unique instrument graphics, and seats with larger side bolsters and distinctive red and black upholstery.

They also employ an asymmetric tread design with the inner tread biased toward wet grip and the outboard areas working best in the dry. In lieu of a spare, a can of high-tech "stop leak" and an inflation kit are supplied.

Finally, to make the most of the increased thrust and grip, Chevrolet engineers took a few things out of the Z06—namely, 38 pounds. About 23 pounds comes from the new tires, thanks to the lack of run-flat reinforcements. Another six or so pounds comes from slightly thinner glass in the windshield and rear window. Finally, the Z06 gets a set of titanium mufflers (see sidebar), which are about 18 pounds lighter than the stainless silencers used on C5s. (Heavier drivetrain and suspension bits offset some of these reductions.)

Since the Z06 Vette only comes in the lightweight hardtop body style—the convertible and hatchback C5s will be powered by the updated LS1 V-8—these

reductions yield a feathery car. Our example weighed 3126 pounds, or 54 pounds less than the last hardtop we tested. That's just 77 pounds more than a BMW M coupe, which is more than 20 inches shorter than the Corvette and five inches narrower and has much smaller rubber and an engine barely half the size.

Although the keen-eyed will pick up on the Z06's new wheels and wider tires, Chevrolet designers gave the new model a few more obvious visual cues. Stainless-steel wire mesh fills the twin grilles in the front fascia, which feed cool air to the new engine. Vents with similar grilles are tacked onto the body just forward of the

The Z06's functional vents are finished with fine-mesh stainless-steel grilles.

COUNTERPOINT

Just 199 '63 Corvettes were built with the previous Z06 package. It fortified the Sting Ray for race duty with a pit-stop-postponing 36.5-gallon gas tank, a stiffer suspension, knock-off wheels, and innovative aluminum drum brakes that were self-adjusting while driving forward. This lightweight race-car starter-kit model will sell more copies, but it'll be an instant collector's item just the same. Its engine note is coarser than the volume model's, and its handling is somewhat cruder, but it's the quickest factory Vette money can buy. Smaller-volume specials like this one are the high-octane fuel that powers the Corvette collecting hobby. Chevy should do one every year.

—Frank Markus

As much as I love the Z06, I'm not sure it vaults the Corvette onto my must-buy list. My must-buy cars are superb all-rounders, with some cargo room, a reasonably comfy ride, and of course, mucho haul-ass-ability. If only Chevy would let me build my Corvette à la carte, I'd sprint to the dealer. Here's my dream Vette: hatchback body; Z06 powertrain, brakes, brake ducts, tires, and various lightweight parts; and Z51 suspension. Notice the last item. The Z06 rides too stiffly for me, but the Z51 package has always struck me as the best ride-and-handling compromise. Too bad it's not available on the Z06, because then I might make do with the hardtop body. *—Larry Webster*

Bulletin: Titanium mufflers do not necessarily make for a mellifluous exhaust. Not if you're addicted to the throbbing baritone of a good ol' American pushrod V-8. Potent as it is—and it *will* distort your face—the LS6 sounds asthmatic below 4500 rpm and thrashy beyond. The rear shocks transmit road noise. The six-speed is a tad clunky. And the independent suspension feels almost *too* independent; on warty roads each corner dances to a slightly different beat, although there's grip galore and the brakes are absolutely world-class. So, give the Z06 a B-minus for refinement. But just try to match this car's visceral rush for the same money. No (expletive deleted) way.

—Tony Swan

Tech Highlight: The Wonder Metal

It's 43 percent less dense than steel but just as strong. It's highly resistant to corrosion. It can be cast, machined, and stamped. So why aren't cars built of titanium?

The purchasing department will be happy to explain why the use of this unique metal is rare. Standard steel costs about 35 cents a pound. The high-strength variety is maybe a buck a pound. And stainless steel is about half again as much. Titanium is in a different league altogether. The alloys used in jet engines cost roughly $15 to $25 per pound. Even a grade suitable for mufflers costs about $10 a pound.

Moreover, although titanium can be stamped like steel, the technique is more demanding, possibly involving the use of heat, but Arvin, the company that makes the Corvette muffler assemblies, won't reveal the details. Titanium must also be welded in a pure argon atmosphere lest oxygen work its way into the weld and weaken it.

As a result, titanium components are very dear. But when you pick up a titanium Corvette muffler, the payoff is clear. It weighs 13 pounds–almost nine pounds less than a muffler made of stainless steel. And it looks trick, with the characteristic dark-gray color that will turn rainbows of purple, blue, and orange with heat and time.

Timet, the supplier of the titanium used in the Corvette's mufflers, is hoping to supply titanium springs as well. Because of the material's strength and stiffness, titanium springs require less wire than steel ones, which combine with the lower density to weigh as much as 75 percent less than a steel spring. The reduced bulk can also reduce hood height or reduce intrusion in a rear suspension on a van or SUV.

With all these advantages, count on seeing the dull-gray sheen of titanium on more cars and trucks in the future. *—CC*

rear wheels to direct cooling air to the rear brakes. Z06 logos are added to the front fenders and instrument cluster and embroidered into the headrests of the specially upholstered seats. Finally, the front and rear brake calipers are painted red, and the titanium mufflers sport larger exhaust tips than do the other '01 models.

More power, more grip, and less weight add up to an infallible prescription for higher performance, and the Z06 fills the bill. Our test car's engine, with just 1400 miles on it, accelerated to 60 mph in 4.3 seconds and covered the quarter-mile in 12.7 seconds at 113 mph. That makes this Z06 half a second quicker than the fastest C5 we've ever tested and quicker than the ZR-1 model that ruled the Corvette roost from 1990 to '95. Among remotely affordable cars, only the Dodge Viper GTS is quicker.

Continuing the drag race to higher speeds, the Z06 attains 150 mph in 28 seconds flat, 0.3 second quicker than the

ZR-1 and 2.4 seconds quicker than the C5. Only in its 168-mph top speed, which is limited by the shorter gearing, does the Z06 give up straight-line speed to the 175-mph ZR-1s and C5s.

The Z06 shuts down all this speed just as ferociously as it creates it, thanks to its wide and sticky tires. Our car stopped from 70 mph in 152 feet—one of the shortest stopping distances we've ever recorded. Most C5s and ZR-1s have required another car length or so to stop from that speed.

The Z06 demonstrates similar superiority in cornering grip: 0.98 g with excellent balance and no twitchiness at the limit. That figure is also one of the best we've ever seen for a production car, ranking about 0.10 g beyond recent Corvettes, as well as edging out the Viper GTS and the Ferrari 360 Modena.

These individual performance strengths coordinated beautifully during a few laps at Mid-Ohio racetrack, where the Z06 felt very much like the Corvette showroom-stock endurance cars that several of us raced in the mid-'80s. A smooth touch on the controls was rewarded with beautiful balance and great stability. And when you do finally exceed the car's limits, the tires seem to smoothly smear across the pavement rather than suddenly break away, providing ample opportunity to retain control.

But the Z06 does not care for the heavy-handed—or -footed. Tromp on the throttle too suddenly while exiting a corner, and the tail will instantly step out—provided you have switched off the active-handling system. Crank coarse motions into the steering wheel, and the Z06 darts around because the steering remains responsive well past the point when most cars are barely hanging on for dear life.

Despite this performance, on the street the Z06 is remarkably docile. The high-output engine is not temperamental, and its increased torque, combined with the shorter gearing, endows the Z06 with highly responsive top-gear acceleration. From 50 to 70 mph in sixth, the Z06's 8.6-second

time was a vast improvement over the 12.0 seconds of the last hardtop we tested.

Despite the stiffer suspension, the ride was reasonably painless over our pock-marked Michigan pavement, thanks to the greater compliance of the non-run-flat tires. However, on lumpy back roads, the Z06 never quite settles down. The rear end bobs around more than we'd like, and when you hit a midcorner bump, the rear tires have a tendency to stutter-step sideways.

Those who want the quickest Corvette however, will likely find the Z06 sufficiently comfortable. Chevrolet expects that 20 percent of Corvette buyers will opt for this model. Prices haven't been set, but expect a bit less than $50,000, with few options. When we recall that the old ZR-1 cost about twice as much as a garden-variety Corvette, that makes the Z06 a bargain—and the perfect model to take the Corvette into the 21st century.

C/D TEST RESULTS

ACCELERATION

	Seconds
Zero to 30 mph	1.8
40 mph	2.5
50 mph	3.5
60 mph	4.3
70 mph	5.6
80 mph	6.8
90 mph	8.2
100 mph	10.0
110 mph	12.0
120 mph	14.3
130 mph	17.2
140 mph	21.2
150 mph	28.0
160 mph	37.7
Street start, 5–60 mph	4.9
Top-gear acceleration, 30–50 mph	9.0
50–70 mph	8.6
Standing ¼-mile	12.7 sec @ 113 mph
Top speed (drag limited)	168 mph

BRAKING
70–0 mph @ impending lockup ....152 ft
Fade ....**none** light moderate heavy

HANDLING
Roadholding, 300-ft-dia skidpad ....0.98 g
Understeer ....**minimal** moderate excessive

FUEL ECONOMY
EPA city driving ....19 mpg
EPA highway driving ....28 mpg
C/D-observed fuel economy ....**17 mpg**

INTERIOR SOUND LEVEL
Idle ....62 dBA
Full-throttle acceleration ....87 dBA
70-mph cruising ....76 dBA
70-mph coasting ....75 dBA

CHEVROLET CORVETTE Z06
Vehicle type: front-engine, rear-wheel-drive, 2-passenger, 2-door coupe

Estimated price as tested: $50,500

Major standard accessories: power steering, windows, driver's seat, and locks; A/C; cruise control; tilting steering wheel; rear defroster

Sound system: Delco AM/FM-stereo radio/CD player, 4 speakers

ENGINE
Type ....V-8, aluminum block and heads
Bore x stroke ....3.90 x 3.62 in, 99.0 x 92.0mm
Displacement ....346 cu in, 5665cc
Compression ratio 10.5:1
Engine-control system ....GM with port fuel injection
Emissions controls ....3-way catalytic converter, feedback air-fuel-ratio control, EGR, auxiliary air pump
Valve gear ....pushrods, hydraulic lifters
Power (SAE net) ....385 bhp @ 6000 rpm
Torque (SAE net) ....385 lb-ft @ 4800 rpm
Redline ....6500 rpm

DRIVETRAIN
Transmission ....6-speed manual
Final-drive ratio ....3.42:1, limited slip

Gear	Ratio	Mph/1000 rpm	Max. test speed
I	2.97	7.4	48 mph (6500 rpm)
II	2.07	10.6	69 mph (6500 rpm)
III	1.43	15.3	100 mph (6500 rpm)
IV	1.00	21.9	143 mph (6500 rpm)
V	0.84	26.1	168 mph (6450 rpm)
VI	0.56	39.2	155 mph (4000 rpm)

DIMENSIONS AND CAPACITIES
Wheelbase ....104.5 in
Track, F/R ....62.4/62.6 in
Length ....179.7 in
Width ....73.6 in
Height ....47.7 in
Frontal area ....21.3 sq ft
Ground clearance ....3.9 in

Curb weight 3126
Weight distribution, F/R 53.5/46.5
Fuel capacity ....18.5 g
Oil capacity 6.5
Water capacity 11.8

CHASSIS/BODY
Type ....full-length frame integral with the bo
Body material ....fiberglass-reinforced plas

INTERIOR
SAE volume, front seat ....52 cu
luggage space ....13 cu
Front seats ....buck
Seat adjustments ...fore and aft, seatback angle, front heig rear heig
Restraint systems, front .....manual 3-point belts, driver a passenger airba
General comfort ....poor fair **good** excelle
Fore-and-aft support ....poor fair **good** excelle
Lateral support ....poor fair good **excelle**

SUSPENSION
F: ....ind, unequal-length control arms, transverse plas leaf spring, anti-roll b
R: ....ind, unequal-length control arms with a toe-control li transverse plastic leaf spring, anti-roll b

STEERING
Type ....rack-and-pinion, power-assist
Turns lock-to-lock 2
Turning circle curb-to-curb 42.3

BRAKES
F: ....12.6 x 1.3-in vented d
R: ....12.6 x 1.3-in vented d
Power assist ....vacuum with anti-lock cont

WHEELS AND TIRES
Wheel size ....F: 9.5 x 17 in, R: 10.5 x 18
Wheel type ....cast alumin
Tires ....Goodyear Eagle F1 SC; F: P265/40ZR-17 9 R: P295/35ZR-18 9
Test inflation pressures, F/R 30/30

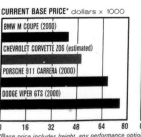

CURRENT BASE PRICE* dollars x 1000
BMW M COUPE (2000)
CHEVROLET CORVETTE Z06 (estimated)
PORSCHE 911 CARRERA (2000)
DODGE VIPER GTS (2000)
0 16 32 48 64 80
*Base price includes freight, any performance options, and all applicable luxury and gas-guzzler taxes.

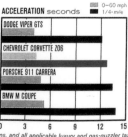

ACCELERATION seconds
0–60 mph
¼-mile
DODGE VIPER GTS
CHEVROLET CORVETTE Z06
PORSCHE 911 CARRERA
BMW M COUPE
0 3 6 9 12 15

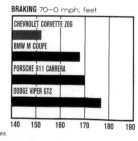

BRAKING 70–0 mph, feet
CHEVROLET CORVETTE Z06
BMW M COUPE
PORSCHE 911 CARRERA
DODGE VIPER GTS
140 150 160 170 180 190

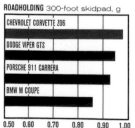

ROADHOLDING 300-foot skidpad, g
CHEVROLET CORVETTE Z06
DODGE VIPER GTS
PORSCHE 911 CARRERA
BMW M COUPE
0.50 0.60 0.70 0.80 0.90 1.00

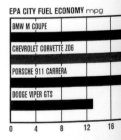

EPA CITY FUEL ECONOMY mpg
BMW M COUPE
CHEVROLET CORVETTE Z06
PORSCHE 911 CARRERA
DODGE VIPER GTS
0 4 8 12 16

Corvette Highs and Lows

How Ford kept the Corvette alive, and how we got Zora his dream job at Chevy.

HIGH The Corvette's savior.

In 1953 and '54, the torpid, two-speed Corvette sold like cold cakes. Then, in '55, Ford poured Drano on GM's wounds with the overnight success of its first sports car, the Thunderbird. Had not GM been humiliated by this turn of events, it certainly would have scuttled the Corvette. So thanks to the T-Bird, GM simply could not call it quits with the Corvette, even though it dearly wanted to.

LOW The fishy work orders.

In January 1985, a *C/D* editor picks up a new Corvette fresh off the assembly line in Bowling Green, Kentucky, and drives it home to Michigan where it will begin a 30,000-mile long-term test. The zoomy Vette is beloved by the speed-geek staff, and the nitpicking is at a whisper, despite numerous faults—electrical failures, a clunky gearshift, a dotty A/C, a leaky window, quickly used-up brake pads, uncooperative wipers. A year and a half later, just days before the car is to be returned, several GM repair orders are found in a back-seat storage bin of the car. The vehicle ID number on the work orders confirms that it is indeed our test car, and the paperwork shows it had been checked out, and repairs made to it, several times at the GM proving ground *before we picked it up*. And, uh, the transmission had been replaced, too. We, of course, squealed to our readers.

LOW 'I say it's got four seats, and I say the hell with it!'

Ford's Thunderbird outsold the Corvette by laughable margins from its first appearance in 1955, and when it became a four-seater in 1958,

Our 40th-birthday baby

PLANET-R/RANDY LORENTZEN

The four-seat Corvette

the T-Bird's sales doubled. So Chevy general manager Ed Cole began considering a four-seat Corvette. Saner minds prevailed—hell, even Chevy's sales promotion manager, usually the last guy to object to this sort of silliness, thought the idea stunk, and said so. But as the radically different '63 Corvette neared its debut, Cole had another four-seat prototype built. One day, GM president Jack Gordon was brought by Styling to have a look. He examined the four-seater, and curious about its roominess, climbed into the back seat. But when the six-foot-two Gordon decided to get out, the front-seat latch broke and the seatback wouldn't flip forward. Help! The boss is trapped! Gordon was extracted and lived to tell the tale,

although the subject of a four-seat Vette was never revisited.

HIGH
The 100-grand Corvette. Ours.

To celebrate *C/D*'s 40th birthday (June 1996), we thought about enrolling the editors in conflict-resolution therapy. Instead, we opted to assemble a Corvette capable of 200 mph, a street-legal one. John Lingenfelter agreed to enlarge an all-aluminum SB2 ("small block, second generation") to a historic 427.6 cubic inches. In this fashion, we obtained modifications valued at $59,991 on a car then valued at $40,061, which added up to a $100,052 Corvette. We were rewarded with 603 horsepower and 554 pound-feet of torque. The car was energetic—we could, for openers, smoke the tires all the way through first and second gears. (Ha-ha. We would never do that more than twice or seven times.) Even on Michelin street tires, our Corvette bolted to 60 mph in 3.6 seconds, turned the quarter in 11.5 at 129 mph, but did not turn the 200 mph we'd hoped for. It turned 212. This meant that our anniversary project was the quickest and fastest U.S. street-legal car we tested in our four-decade history, although in cost-consciousness, it was Enron on wheels.

LOW John Z.'s better idea.

Wonder boy John Z. De Lorean, fresh from the Pontiac Motor Division where he's created the GTO, the Grand Prix, and a glamorous image for himself, arrives at Chevy as general manager in 1969. Wow, the guy's only 44! He gets an idea that will turbocharge his climb to corporate destiny among GM's layers of beancounters and brass: Build the Corvette on the same platform as the Camaro, and save big bucks! Then John Z. explained that the Vette's notorious quality problems were not in the car's design but in the plant. "St. Louis was one of the worst plants that GM had," he said. "Nobody wanted the foreman job. They were afraid someone would beat them up and slash their tires." These are the same guys that laughed at the assembly-line memoir *Rivethead.* Wisely, De Lorean brought the plant up to standard within a year and dropped the idea of the platform sharing.

A Corvette stinker

LOW They meant *Corvette Bummer.*

Here's the plot of the 1978 flick *Corvette Summer:* A kid restores a Vette in shop class, has it stolen, and later goes to Las Vegas to retrieve it, where he falls in love with a whore. Hey, happens around here all the time, but still, whoever mutilated this perfectly good Corvette oughtta be kneecapped. By the way, this stinker starred Mark Hamill, who just a year earlier headlined in *Star Wars,* the highest-grossing film at the time.

HIGH Get your kicks.

Route 66 ran for an hour on TV Friday nights from October 7, 1960, until September 1964. It was a fantasy road-trip series beloved by teenage boys dying to break the bonds of home, and it starred Martin Milner as Tod Stiles (runner-up for the part was yet another blond surfer type named Robert Redford), a nice rich kid with a Corvette, and George Maharis as Buz Murdock, a moody, tough kid from

HIGH We get Zora his dream job . . .

GM in the '50s and '60s studiously kept the volatile Russian engineer Zora Arkus-Duntov from gaining full control over at the Corvetteworks. His title was "director of high performance" for Chevy, whatever that meant. Duntov was always haranguing the lords of the manor to let him build a mid-engined, Ferrari-killing Corvette, while GM was happy to take the low road (and the high cash) and told Zora to watch his mouth. Finally, in the spring of '67, Chevy general manager Pete Estes yanked Duntov out of the Corvette shop altogether, making the brilliant if self-promoting engineer a *PR man!* Meantime, the Vette's shoddy workmanship continued, and GM had no backstop. Eight months later, in a column in the December 1967 issue of *Car and Driver,* editor Steve Smith told readers that a '68 Corvette test car's "shocking lack of quality control" was so bad the magazine was, in disgust, refusing to

New York who wandered America meddling in other people's business. Shows were shot on location from Montana to Florida, in places that were genuinely different from the homogenized country we live in today. Chevy was glad to donate, first off, a Horizon Blue '60 Corvette, followed by a Fawn Beige model in '61. After that, they were all brown. Maharis got a black fuel-injected model but switched to a carbureted car because deep-woods mechanics were baffled by the fuelie. Milner was the family man and drove a Chevy wagon off-screen. The crew of 40 to 60 spent 254 days away from home the first year and had gone 80,000 miles by the end of the second season, passing through 36 states. By season three, Maharis bailed

GRAND ISLE II

Buz and Tod, busybodies

test it. Smith used up a whole column railing about all the idiot defects in the car. Estes, proving he could read, did a 180, and Duntov was finally made chief engineer at Corvette. Years later, Duntov would acknowledge, "Steve Smith's article is what nailed it down."

LOW . . . and he thanks us with a lawsuit!

Now it's 1979. *Car and Driver* columnist Don Sherman, who says he can produce engineering degrees from University of Iowa and University of Michigan if pushed, has the gall to express an opinion about an aspect of the Corvette's engineering that he determines to be less than perfection. Really going for the jugular, Sherman opines in print that the Corvette's rear suspension, *from 1963 onward,* was "ill-conceived." Duntov, by now obviously a lifetime subscriber to the magazine that got him his job, reads Sherman's remarks—*and promptly sues us!*

out for a bigger contract (citing hepatiti Plans to shoot *Route 66* in Europe, whi would have been a real hoot back then, f apart.

LOW The sinking, stinking '70s.

In 1971, a base Corvette had 270 hors power and came with a four-speed manu If you had $1221 lying around, you cou jack up the horsepower to *425.* By mi decade, all that would change, a although sales boomed, Chevy turned back on the joys of power. In 1975, t base car had sunk to a pitiful 165 hors (the only engine option raised that to dubious 205). The convertible was se into exile that year, not to return until '8 In 1976, buyers in California were deni a manual transmission. St Corvettes sold like cra from 38,465 in '75 to 46,5 the next year, despite a h hum 180-hp base car (o 210-hp option). In '71, t base car cost $5496; 10 ye later it was $16,259, nea triple the price.

True, a big chunk of t power loss was due to t change from SAE gross to ratings in '72, but we still g huffy about it. Yates wro "Buying a Corvette is l

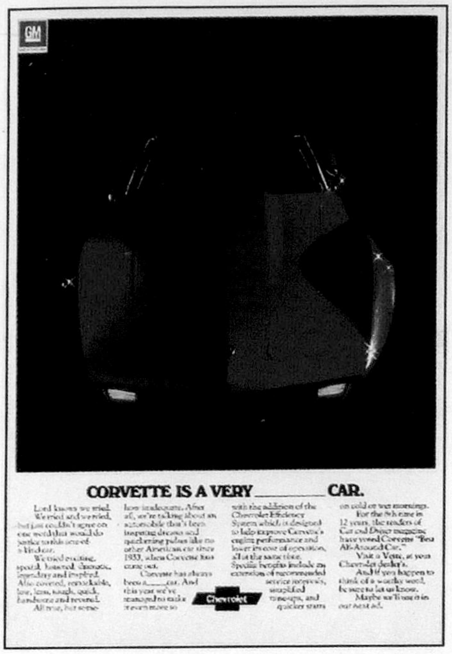

joining the Elks. It's a young man's version of the Airstream trailer." Bedard sneered at the 190-hp car of 1980: "Ten years ago the typical Corvette spent Saturday morning with its hood up, the engine getting a fine-tune for the street racing that would inevitably follow. Now the typical Corvette rolls up at the country club on Saturday morning, driven by a guy with white shoes and a white belt." With nothing else to do, we compared it with a Bricklin, determining that "women fall hopelessly in love from two lanes away"—*and we were talking about the Bricklin.* And still Chevy sold every one it could make, rising to an all-time high in 1979 of 53,807 units sold, and not one of them in the form of the original: the topless roadster.

LOW Where else can you get this stuff? Crash-testing a Corvette.

In 1969, *C/D* writer Charles Fox got in over his head and crashed an expensive Can-Am car. We exploited his embarrassing misfortune with a cover blurb that sounded like we'd turned into safety geeks: "Crash-Testing a Can-Am Car." In '87, tech editor Csaba Csere provided us with a second opportunity when he drove a Powell Motorsports Corvette in a 24-hour race at Mosport in Ontario. During a yellow, teammate Paul Tracy pulled in and turned over the wheel to Csere, who tore out before the pack, which was cruising along behind the pace car, could lap him. Trying to catch them, he flew through the right-hander at the end of the pits and entered a fast, downhill, off-camber turn carrying, as they say, a bit too much speed. "Next thing I knew I was sideways at about 90 mph, onto the wide grass runoff, where I spun around and smacked the tire wall—driver side first—so hard that the compressed tires bounced the Vette about two feet into the air on the rebound." The car looked like bad taffy. "I was so mortified that I'd thrown the car away during a yellow that I didn't remove my helmet as I walked back, hoping no one would recognize me." This never happens at *Consumer Reports.*

LOW The missing model year.

In the fall of 1982, the traditional new-car season, we wandered over to the Corvette tent at Chevy . . . and found it empty. *Say what? Who the hell's in charge here!?* As a result, there's no such thing as a *1983* Corvette. Doesn't exist. Chevy simply didn't get it done in time—in fact, it didn't turn up until a half-year later, in March 1983. Chevy general manager Bob Stempel, whose brief and unlucky reign later as GM's chairman was filled with this sort of nightmare bad luck, simply called it a 1984 Corvette. (By the way, we used this strategy in missing April's tax deadline. We're gonna tell the IRS we'll do it next year.)

HIGH Beef: It's what's for dinner!

The go-go '80s were in their last throes when GM decided it was time to put some go-go back into its Corvette. The 1990 ZR-1 Vette arrived with four overhead cams, 32 valves, a bunch of aluminum, 375 horsepower (the base model had 250), fatter wheels and tires, a *mandatory* manual (yes!), and sound-system goodies. Power was back! We were ecstatic! At least up to the moment we discovered the ZR-1 was priced at

Corvette ZR-1

DAVID DEWHURST

$27,016 more than a base Corvette's already swollen sticker of $31,979 (yes, that's $58,995 total). That may have had something to do with the fact that just 6939 ZR-1s were sold by the time the model faded out in 1995.

HIGH So, when's the big ticker-tape parade?

We've heard the vicious whispering for five decades: As race cars, Corvettes make nice ashtrays. The whispers usually come in German, British, and Italian accents. Oh, yeah? In 2001, a 620-hp Chevy Corvette, built by Pratt & Miller, not only survived the hellish 24 hours of Daytona over 2335 miles but in fact bagged an overall victory! The winning drivers were Ron Fellows, Franck Freon, Johnny O'Connell, and Chris Kneifel, none of whom has yet to be invited to celebrity night on *The Weakest Link.*

A big winner at last

Dead-End Vettes

Some show cars had startling innovations and new ideas but wound up ignored and discarded.

BY WALLACE A. WYSS

1954 Corvair

▲ Yeah, we know, the production Corvair came along in 1960, but the name appeared in '54 on a fastback Corvette concept that had shades of Euro influence atop an American-as-apple-pie design. It wasn't until the '63 Sting Ray coupe that Chevrolet added a fixed-roof version to supplement the convertible. Sports-car fans who felt convertibles were "flexi-fliers" and preferred the rigidity of a coupe rejoiced.

1954 Corvette Nomad

▶ This GM Motorama show car was a station wagon from the windshield back and a Corvette from the windshield forward. It wasn't concocted from a stock '53 Corvette—it has the first-generation nose installed on a steel station-wagon body. Why wasn't it ever slated for production? If Chevy could barely sell 300 Corvettes in that first year of 1953, one model was more than enough—and who wants a sports-car station wagon anyway? When the same roof style was sent over to the Chevy lineup of cars, the division had a hit for three years in the Nomad wagon.

1964 CERV II

◀ Back in the 1930s, Zora Arkus-Duntov was a Russian student of engineering in Germany. He wrote to Auto Union to inform the firm that he was a full convert to its mid-engined V-12 and V-16 racing cars, which would need four-wheel drive if they expected to get all that power to the pavement. He was round-filed, of course. Flash forward 30 or so years. As the director of high performance at Chevrolet, Duntov had the budget to build an R&D car. So what was his approach? A mid-engined four-wheel-drive car, roughly along the lines of a sports-racing car. (So close, in fact, that it was lent secretly to Chaparral for a joint development program on the Texas team's endurance racer.) Duntov was way ahead of the curve on this one, fitting the CERV II with a pair of two-speed automatic gearboxes driving all four wheels. Today you can buy a Porsche, an Audi, or a number of other four-wheel-drive high-performance cars. GM let both the idea and the concept car get away, and today the CERV II is owned by a Cincinnati collector.

KURTIS OBLINGER

1970 XP-882

▲ A Duntov tour de force was his engineering of this mid-engined Corvette. Not just mid-engined, mind you—the 400-cubic-inch V-8 was placed sideways, à la Lamborghini Miura. This kept the weight more inside the axles for a lower polar moment of inertia (translating to more agile cornering). Drive was routed through a Turbo Hydra-matic transmission mounted parallel to and forward of the engine, then turned 90 degrees and routed aft through the oil pan to the rear differential—all of which allowed the engine to be lowered dramatically. It was so fiendishly clever that Duntov was granted three patents on the engineering. GM styling boss Bill Mitchell added the teardrop rear roof shape, reminiscent of the 1963–67 Sting Ray coupe—a design cue that might come back if GM goes retro on the next-generation Corvette (see story on page 72).

1972 XP-895

◀ GM Design had done the XP-882 in fiberglass, then a redesign in steel, but supplier Reynolds Aluminum, always trying to land the big contract, offered to do an identical reskin in aluminum to prove its feasibility. GM handed over a spare chassis, and an outside vendor did the reskin. The styling of the "Reynolds Corvette" delivered a fresh take on the '68 Corvette tunnel-back ("sugar scoop") roof and a more contemporary look overall. The weight was way down, but Reynolds' alchemists couldn't devise a way to build an aluminum body as inexpensively as a fiberglass one. So fiberglass continued to be the norm. Decades later, Honda's Acura Division would go the all-aluminum route with its NSX sports car.

1973 Two-Rotor

▲ As Marlon Brando complained in *On the Waterfront,* "I coulda been a contendah." This design coulda been, too—penned at GM but bodied in Italy by Pininfarina and fitted to a Porsche 914 chassis. The XP-897GT two-rotor was originally an Opel project, a study for taking on Porsche in the luxury sports-car field. In Detroit, GM president Ed Cole saw an opportunity to get some attention for the new rotary-engine powerplant and had it installed. A sweet deal it was. With a 2.2-liter engine (larger even than the Mazda three-rotor), the car was a rorty little runner, as we found out on a brief drive. Duntov, however, was unsatisfied with its performance, and the concept died along with the rotary engine at GM.

The First Corvette

Thank you, Mrs. Brooks,
wherever you are.

BY TONY SWAN

I t's very appealing to think that the Corvette sprang fully formed from the brow of GM styling czar Harley Earl one spring evening in 1952, just like Athena materializing from the forehead of Zeus. The mythological parallel is appropriate, because at that stage of his career Earl's pronouncements on auto cosmetics were pretty much regarded as divine.

But history doesn't work like that. Before there could be a Corvette, there had to be precursors—other sports cars. There weren't many of them in post–World War II America—a few MGs and Jaguars, a handful of Allards. The GM vision of a sporty two-seater was mani-

fested in the Le Sabre and Buick XP-300, conjured up for GM's Motorama dream-car road show. Big, ponderous, and bechromed, they were the antithesis of the

They're standing on a Glasspar-bodied car to show the toughness of plastic. The company sold sports-car kits to fit over 1939–48 Ford and Mercury running gear. The plastic car's design strongly influenced the Corvette.

sports-car ethos—that is, a car that could be as much at home in a road race as on a boulevard. Earl's own notion of a sports car revolved vaguely around the Willys Jeepster.

That notion was prophetic, because a Jeep figured in the Corvette's inspiration. According to Karl Ludvigsen's authoritative narrative *Corvette: America's Star-Spangled Sports Car, The Complete History* (Automobile Quarterly Publications/ E.P. Dutton & Co., New York, 1973), the story began in 1950 when Air Force Maj. Kenneth B. Brooks presented his wife with a Jeep. To his surprise, she refused to be seen in it: SUVs weren't quite ready for prime time in 1950.

Dismayed, Brooks commissioned Bill [Tr]itt, a founder of Glasspar Boats, to fab[ric]ate a fiberglass roadster body that could [be] attached to the Jeep chassis. Tritt did [ju]st that, creating a handsome two-seater [wi]th strong Jaguar XK120 overtones.

Fiberglass—more accurately known as [gl]ass-reinforced plastic, or GRP—was still [in] its infancy at the time. When the re[bo]died Jeep was reborn as the Brooks [Bo]xer, it attracted the attention of the Nau[ga]tuck Chemical Division of U.S. Rubber. [Na]ugatuck had been trying unsuccessfully [to] sell Detroit automakers on the virtues of [G]RP, but the Boxer, acquired by the com[pa]ny as a promotional tool, changed the cli[m]ate dramatically. In March 1952, Nau[ga]tuck sales executive Earl Ebers drove the [ca]r to the National Plastics Exposition in [Ph]iladelphia, where Chevy engineers [de]scended on the new shape, wanting more [inf]o on the new body material.

[F]rom Philadelphia, Ebers took the car [to] Detroit, where it was rolled into the [pre]sence of Earl himself. The great man [lik]ed what he saw.

[A]lthough the Tritt design helped [sh]arpen Earl's sports-car focus, a good many other players were involved in shaping the Corvette's design. For example, Cal Tech grad Robert F. McLean was responsible for the chassis layout. Contrary to prevailing convention, McLean started at the rear axle and worked forward. His aim was to have the passenger compartment well aft, with the engine close to the fire wall, for favorable weight distribution. This in turn dictated the classic sports-car proportions.

It also meant the Corvette wouldn't be just a rebodied version of a standard Chevrolet sedan. The frame and the 102-inch wheelbase were unique to the sports car, although the front suspension, the Blue Flame Six engine, and the Powerglide two-speed automatic all came from the Chevy parts bin. With three single-throat carbs, a bit more compression, a high-lift cam, and other mods, the 235.5-cubic-inch OHV straight-six went from 115 horsepower to 150. But allied with the Powerglide automatic, its performance was still tepid, even by the modest standards of the day.

Maurice Olley was responsible for the Corvette's chassis development, and Ed Cole, newly appointed as Chevy's chief engineer, involved himself in powertrain issues. Meanwhile, Earl appointed a styling task force to wrap the hardware in GRP. Vincent Kaptur was responsible for body engineering, draftsman Carl Peebles rendered Earl's ideas into lines on paper, Bill Bloch assisted Peebles, clay modeler Tony Balthasar translated the drawings into a three-dimensional shape, and Joe Schemansky handled the interior, including the low-set row of secondary gauges that looked so cool and were so hard to read.

By June 1952, a full-size plaster model was approved for showing on the 1953 GM Motorama circuit, which kicked off in January at New York's Waldorf-Astoria. By that time at least one running prototype was undergoing evaluation at GM's proving ground in Milford, Michigan, and by June production was under way at a temporary facility in Flint, Michigan.

It is not recorded whether Mrs. Brooks ever got her original Jeep-based roadster back. But we're glad the SUV infatuation was still well over the horizon when her husband came home with that new Jeep.

Tweaks to Chevy's Blue Flame Six bumped horsepower to 150, but the '53 Vette was still a sluggish sports car.

The Corvette has always been about ego and power, on the part of its owners as well as its creators. One of the more legendary battles in this respect took place in the early 1960s between design staff chief Bill Mitchell and Corvette engineer Zora Arkus-Duntov over control of the shape and drivetrain configuration of the Corvette Sting Ray, the first all-new Corvette since 1953. Now, in this modified excerpt from Jerry Burton's recently published biography, Zora Arkus-Duntov: The Legend Behind Corvette, *we find that the Sting Ray was not exactly the car Duntov wanted to build.*

Zora's quest to make his mark at GM would extend, inevitably, to creating his own Corvette. Despite the lack of any real authority, he had already exerted a major influence on the existing car. Little by little, his project assignments for engineers Maurice Olley, Ed Cole, and Harry Barr had yielded a Corvette that Zora proudly deemed "a dog no longer." The 1961 and 1962 models represented significant performance increases, with more power thanks to a standard 250-hp 327, and as much as 360 horsepower on tap via a fuel-injected version. Despite more guts and a new ducktail rear end, the basic chassis and layout remained unchanged from 1953, including an unsophisticated solid rear axle. In Zora's eyes, that represented a severe limitation to the Corvette's performance potential.

Duntov knew the Corvette needed an all-new design, and he had one in mind— a machine that represented everything he had learned about engineering in his 50-plus years. Based on his experiences with the CERV I (Chevrolet Engineering Research Vehicle I), a provocative open-wheel race car, and the Q Corvette, a concept pushed by then Chevrolet chief engineer Ed Cole that called for a transaxle just like that of today's C5 Corvette, Duntov saw the opportunity to build a mid-engined machine that would rank among the world's finest sports cars at any price.

But the keys to the Corvette kingdom at General Motors were not so easily obtained. The Corvette had also aroused the passion of Harley Earl's successors in the design staff who had their own ideas about a fitting replacement for Earl's original Corvette. The design staff enjoyed a preeminent position within the corporation. Thanks to Earl's expressive postwar designs, appearance had become more important than engineering. Design provided the sizzle, often obscuring warmed-

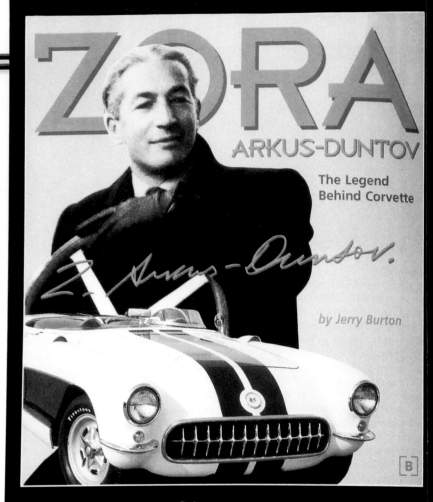

The Struggle over the Sting Ray

Corvette patron saint Zora Arkus-Duntov and GM design chief Bill Mitchell faced off in the early 1960s over who ruled the Corvette roost. The outcome of that battle defines the plastic two-seater of today.

BY JERRY BURTON

over underpinnings in the 1950s and 1960s.

Indeed, a race to control the future direction of the Corvette was shaping up between Chevy engineering and the design staff, and Zora was squarely on the front lines. His opponent would be Bill Mitchell, Earl's successor as vice-president of design. Like Earl, Mitchell was an iconoclast. Fiercely independent and opinionated, he lived and breathed fast machinery, be it jet airplanes, motorcycles, or automobiles. He was a commanding presence with his large round face, long sideburns, and bald crown.

Mitchell already had a design theme in mind for the next-generation Corvette. Back in 1957, he created a styling theme for the clay-model Q Corvette that was inspired by a series of Pininfarina and Boano bodies built on Italian Abarths, according to Karl Ludvigsen in his book *Corvette: America's Star-Spangled Sports Car.* Mitchell was particularly influenced by one record speed car that he had seen at the Turin motor show in 1957. The car had a wedge shape characterized by a sharp crease around its perimeter. Bulges were incorporated above the wheel wells to accommodate the tires within the relatively flat top shape of the car.

Mitchell was so taken by the Abarth that he brought back photos of it from Italy and showed them to his key designers, who included Chuck Pohlmann, Tony Lapine, Pete Brock, and Bob Veryzer. According to Ludvigsen, Mitchell challenged each of them to try their own variations of the Abarth as a possible candidate to become the Q Corvette. Mitchell's team took this basic look and added a fastback roofline and an extreme wedge-shaped front end. For its time, the Q Corvette was a stunning new direction for Chevrolet's sports car. However, management considered it too costly to produce, owing to its novel powertrain and rear-mounted transmission, and it was canceled in 1958.

In 1959, Mitchell, now head of the GM design staff, had the opportunity to revive and expand upon the Q theme by creating a special race-car body. The body was designed by Pohlmann and Brock under Mitchell's direction and was engineered to fit over the chassis of Zora's SS mule car, which had been mothballed since GM pulled the racing plug in 1957. Mitchell decided to race the car to test public reaction to this revolutionary design theme. When it was all done, its sleek design suggested a graceful yet evil sea creature. Mitchell

named it the Sting Ray even though it was a shark that had inspired it.

Duntov was nervous about the whole project for several reasons. Because of the corporate ban on racing, he had no control over the effort. This was strictly a private affair staffed by volunteer engineers and design staff personnel such as Larry Shinoda (whose distinguished career would eventually include the Camaro Z28 and the Boss 302 Mustang). Second, as a race car, the Sting Ray wasn't any more advanced than the original SS and suffered from many of the same problems, including bad brakes. Aerodynamically, it might have been worse than the SS, as the body actually created lift instead of downforce. Since the car's underpinnings were still his own design and he didn't want a project he had no connection with to come back and haunt him, Duntov tried to prevent Mitchell from obtaining the SS mule. More fundamentally, he didn't want Mitchell running a project—officially or unofficially—with the name Corvette attached to it. He was unsuccessful. As a General Motors vice-president, Mitchell simply had too much clout.

Zora's fears were justified, not because the Sting Ray would be an embarrassment on the track for GM, but because of the momentum its success would create. The Sting Ray racer proved what a good car the SS actually was, for it was not only competitive but also a winner. The car propelled Dick Thompson to the Sports Car Club of America C-Modified National Championship in 1959. Thompson also won the same championship in 1960 before Mitchell retired the car to the auto-show circuit.

Buoyed by wild public enthusiasm for the design, Mitchell had Shinoda execute the adaptation of the Sting Ray into a pro-

duction Corvette. This move set the mold for the second-generation Corvette to become a front-engined car, a fact that had Duntov fuming. He never liked the long-hooded look of the Sting Ray racer because it interfered with forward visibility. He had been frustrated with the efforts of Mitchell and his designers in trying to design a body for a mid-engined car back in the late 1950s. Both Lapine and Shinoda were assigned by Mitchell to work with Duntov on some early concepts, but their direction from Mitchell was to maintain a long hood. According to Duntov, the end result provided no indication that they were creating a mid-engined car: "I thought that external design should reflect what the car is." Accordingly, Duntov thought Mitchell's idea of car design was frozen in 1937 with the long hood of the Mercedes SS or Duesenberg J.

The working prototype for the production Corvette was called the XP-720, which bore an immediate resemblance to the Sting Ray racer. Making matters worse for Zora was another design element added to the XP-720 that would become the trademark of the Sting Ray—a tapered fastback hardtop. It featured a wind split that ran down the center of the car in an uninterrupted line from the windshield to the rear deck.

Mitchell borrowed this concept from Harley Earl's Golden Rocket show car of 1956, which was built along the whimsical rocket/aviation theme expressed in such vehicles as the GM XP-500 and Firebird show cars. Mitchell's execution, to be sure, was far more aesthetically pleasing, but it still necessitated dividing the back window, which obscured rear visibility. When it was first designed, the split was narrower than in the actual production version. But the engineers widened it so they could get more structure into the glass seals. No matter how wide or narrow the split, for Zora such an intrusion into the driving function was an issue worthy of war.

So Duntov challenged Mitchell directly, venturing into the inner sanctum of GM Design to air his displeasure. He was on sacred ground. Never before had an engineer, especially one with so little authority on such a

Duntov went to war with Bill Mitchell over the '63 Sting Ray's split window. Duntov felt the split obscured rear visibility.

low-volume car line, had the audacity to blow smoke into the face of kings like Bill Mitchell.

Duntov was out to shift the balance between styling and engineering back toward engineering. But he was one man on a limited-volume car line without a mandate from his superiors. He had his work cut out for him.

Duntov recalled looking at an early prototype of the XP-720 in the GM styling dome with Bill Mitchell. "We are sitting there, and Bill was squinting at the car and said, 'Ah, look at it. You see the blood, the blood streaming out of the mouth of the car—like big fish.'"

But blood was about to be spilled over the issue of the split window. *"My* blood," said Zora in a 1992 issue of *Corvette Quarterly.* Duntov hated the split window for the same reason he hated the long hood—it obstructed the driver's view.

Meadow Brook Hall concours founder and former GM stylist Dave Holls once said that Duntov's visit to the design department was "like a Lutheran visiting the Vatican." He was in a foreign place. Mitchell was aghast at the idea that an engineer would challenge him on his own turf, and as a result there were some serious words, even shouting. "Mitchell got very red-faced during these discussions," recalled Chuck Jordan, GM's design chief from 1986 through 1992, who witnessed many of the arguments.

"Mitchell would say, 'I'm the designer, and you're the engineer, and engineering never sold a goddamn thing,'" said Shinoda, who was also present for the discussions. "Knowing it pissed him off, Mitchell would call Duntov 'Zorro' or sometimes just a 'fucking white Russian.' Zora, in turn, called Mitchell 'a red-faced baboon.'"

Mitchell used whatever leverage he felt he could get away with, suggesting he could pull the plug on the independent rear suspension or other engineering goodies Duntov had in mind for the car. Whether Mitchell had the kind of corporate muscle to control the engineering content of the car was something Zora

didn't want to find out. So Duntov took the matter to Ed Cole, then Chevrolet general manager. But Cole decided to compromise and let Mitchell have his split window for at least the first year.

Duntov exacted a measure of revenge when it came to deciding who would be allowed to drive early Sting Ray prototypes from engineering. According to Ludvigsen, among those *not* on the list was Mitchell. And Mitchell's ego was big enough not to stand pat. So he built his own car, inspired by a shark he caught on vacation off Bimini. The new car was based on a 1962 chassis and was a successor to the XP-700 show car that first showcased the ducktail look.

Mitchell's new car, the XP-755 (later called the Mako Shark), featured the Sting Ray look but had a more overt shark theme with gills on the front quarter-panels and graded coloration ranging from a white underbody to a dark, iridescent blue on the hood and rear deck. Mitchell's Mako became one of the most popular and memorable of all the Corvette show cars. Ironically, the Mako Shark—designed as a convertible with a clear bubble top—never had a split window.

The split-window issue stuck in Duntov's craw long after the street Sting Ray went into production. He had taken his strongest stand on an issue since he had joined the corporation—and lost. Duntov earned the longer-term victory, however, and the split disappeared after the 1963 model year. What factors ultimately resulted in the decision are not documented, but Zora's opposition combined with scornful reviews from the enthusiast media may have been enough to kill it. Ironically, cost issues may have contributed to the demise of the split window as well, since it was cheaper to manufacture and install one rear window for the fastback rather than two.

Despite the controversy over

GM design chief Bill Mitchell poses with his Sting Ray racer, which established the design direction for the 1963 Corvette.

the split window, the impact of the Sting Ray on the world market was nothing short of remarkable. The car literally stopped people in their tracks. Most historians agree that it was the best Corvette design ever, the standard by which any new design is measured. But not everyone in the design staff was convinced the Sting Ray was perfect. "I always thought the Sting Ray had too many phony scoops, especially compared with the beautiful E-type Jaguar," said Holls. "Mitchell told me to 'stop worrying about that fucking Jaguar.' He told me that Harley Earl taught him there should be entertainment everywhere you look around the car."

Much to Zora's satisfaction, many 1963 Corvette owners removed the split window, replacing it with a solid piece of glass.

"After the big pissing contest, Zora was sort of banned from styling," said Shinoda. "When Zora did the Grand Sport [a special racing version of the Sting Ray] and he needed my help, he really couldn't ask. I would bootleg stuff out the back door."

Zora clashed again with Mitchell in 1966 and 1967 as the third-generation car was being developed. Zora once again preferred a mid-engine design, while Mitchell was pushing a production version of his Mako Shark II show car built on the same chassis as the 1963. Mitchell again won out.

Years later, at Duntov's retirement party in January 1975, Mitchell stayed away from any overt references to their famous run-ins over the 1963 split-window Sting Ray. Instead, he sought common ground with Zora, referencing the fact that the auto business had become overwrought with restrictions and regulations, which made Mitchell appreciate the value of Zora even more. "With all the restrictions we have today, we need some romance in the business. And thank God we have the Corvette, and thank God, Zora, you've put into the Corvette what made it go."

But Zora wanted to be known for more than making Mitchell's designs "go." And although Duntov had cast his own indelible mark on General Motors and the Corvette, the fact is he lost the war to Mitchell. Had Duntov been more successful, the look and configuration of the Corvettes we drive today—right or wrong—might have been considerably different. •

Jerry Burton is the editorial director of Corvette Quarterly *magazine. His book* Zora Arkus-Duntov: The Legend Behind Corvette *is available through Bentley Publishers, 1734 Massachusetts Avenue, Cambridge, Massachusetts 02138; 800–423–4595; www.bentleypublishers.com.*

Best Premium Sports Car in Initial Quality. Two years in a row.

Once again, J.D. Power and Associates has ranked the Chevrolet® Corvette® highest in initial quality.

It's a powerful tribute to the quality people at GM® who engineer and build them. And it comes as no

surprise to the people who drive one. They win, every time they get behind the wheel. corvette.com

CHEVROLET CORVETTE

PREVIEW 2005 CHEVROLET CORVETTE

Thorough tweaking results in Corvette C5 and 11/16ths.

BY DANIEL PUND

PHOTOGRAPHY BY JIM WEDLAKE

Forget about calling the new Corvette the C6. C6 is something you are afflicted with on a rough sea passage.

Besides, the 2005 Corvette that Chevy unveiled at the Detroit show last month, and which goes on sale in targa and convertible forms late this summer, is hardly the beginning of a new generation, as "C6" would imply. Like the '68 Vette, the 2005 is a profound evolution of the existing car. It's one long stride on the road of continual improvement.

The Corvette's technical daddy, Dave Hill, says 70 percent of the parts numbers are new. We frequently go through this with manufacturers. If the suspension control arms look exactly the same but carry a different parts number, are they new?

We'll compromise and say the 2005 Corvette is the C5 and 11/16ths.

Whatever. As Hill puts it, "The more you look, the more you see."

Which is good, because when they pulled the drape off a bright red 2005 at GM headquarters, we were, let's say, underwhelmed. Of course we were looking at it in profile where the least amount of difference is immediately noticeable. The basic C5 forms are all represented here: Big butt. Pointy nose. Tapered canopy greenhouse.

But there's . . . something different here. It looks more purposeful, more potent, and more compact. It's not entirely a trick of styling. The Corvette has shrunk by five inches in length and by an inch in

width, measured at its still-ample hips. All that length was taken out of the overhangs: two inches from the front and, mercifully, three off the chunky rump. A strengthened crash structure up front allowed the nose job. Rerouting the exhaust straight out the back and placing the mufflers in an area formerly taken up by a useless spare-tire well (that never carried a spare) allowed designers to chop the rear. The C6's wheelbase is 1.2 inches longer than that of the C5. This pushes the wheels to the corners and makes the overall package appear less massive. Those wheels are also larger in diameter by an inch front and rear (18 inches in front; 19 at the rear), which appears to further shrink the body.

But it's the nose and tail that are the obvious dif-

exemplary for its high stiffness at a relatively light weight, remains the same—hydroformed steel side rails, a tall center tunnel, balsa sandwiches for the floors. Likewise, the cast aluminum upper and lower control arms and transverse composite leaf springs are familiar from the C5 and the Cadillac XLR hardtop roadster.

As ever, three suspension variations will be available. The base, or FE1, is not much different from the outgoing car's, although the company claims higher lateral acceleration limits and better on-center steering feel. All Corvette targas and convertibles will also offer the same optional electronically adjusted magnetic shocks that impressed last year on the 50th-anniversary Vette. The big change is in the Z51 sport package, which always came with bigger anti-roll bars and stiffer shocks and springs. For 2005, it comes with all those things plus its own set of tires (which are the same size as the base tire but with an asymmetric tread design and less void space), cross-drilled brake rotors that are larger by about an inch, high-performance brake-pad linings, and the shorter gearing of the current Z06's six-speed manual transaxle.

The six-speed is the same Tremec T-56 unit familiar from the C5, but internal improvements promise better shift quality for all '05 Vettes. If you choose an automatic, it will be the same four-speed as before (the XLR's five-speed auto cannot handle the Corvette's torque), although it now has an adaptive shift algorithm. Hill places the new Z51 in context by saying, "If the Z06 was four seconds a lap faster than a base C5, the new Z51 takes back three of those seconds."

This is due in large part to the new LS2 engine. Chevrolet bored out the aluminum V-8 from 5.7 liters to a nice round 6.0 liters. Each cylinder of the siamese-bore engine is now 101.6 millimeters across, instead of 99. Chevy also increased the compression ratio from 10.1:1 to 10.9:1, raised the redline from 6000 to 6500, substituted a cam with greater lift, and added a freer-flowing induction system and an exhaust with 10-percent-less back pressure. The result is 400 horsepower at 6000 rpm—a 50-hp increase

ference here. The size and shape of the C5's tail was determined more by the wind tunnel than aesthetic considerations, and, well, not everything the wind creates is beautiful. The new tail is still a sharp-edged quasi Kammback, but it tapers a bit more between the trailing edge of the rear wheel and the terminus. Viewed in profile, there's a sort-of S-curve contour that brings some visual interest to the formerly billboard-bland expanse of bum.

Even at first glance the nose of the new car might seem familiar—but not with any previous Corvette. The clear-lens-covered high-intensity-discharge headlamps and low center grille might remind you of the Ferrari 575M Maranello. If you stare at the snout long enough, you will see many things, as Hill had promised. One of them might be a Dodge Viper. The look might not scream Corvette, but it is handsome. The folks at team Corvette are more than aware of their car's vaguely cultlike following, and ditching the hidden headlamps (the first Vette since 1962 without

them) was the source of no small amount of consternation. The new light housings, though, save "some good little amount of weight," allow for the use of HID lamps, and are not "air brakes," as Hill describes the pop-ups.

Unlike the new Mustang (page 48), the Corvette doesn't plagiarize its own past. There's no split rear window as on the '63. No "stinger hood" à la big-block '67s.

But head designer Tom Peters did add a hint of the 1963–67 Sting Ray front and rear fenders. The sharp-edged, tall fenders defined those mid-years Vettes. Think of the 2005's fenders as a version of the C5's fenders but with a good trouser crease running along the tops and slightly into the door panels. Truth is, we didn't even notice them for a few minutes. No surface of the new car has gone untouched, but none looks completely rethought, either.

Underneath the plastic body, the look is even more familiar. The structure, which on the C5 was

2005 CHEVROLET CORVETTE

Vehicle type: front-engine, rear-wheel-drive, 2-passenger, 3-door targa

Estimated base price: $45,000

ENGINE

Type	V-8, aluminum block and heads
Bore x stroke	4.00 x 3.62 in, 101.6 x 92.0 mm
Displacement	364 cu in, 5964cc
Compression ratio	10.9:1
Fuel-delivery system	port injection
Valve gear	pushrods, 2 valves per cylinder, hydraulic lifters
Power (SAE net)	400 bhp @ 6000 rpm
Torque (SAE net)	400 lb-ft @ 4400 rpm
Redline	6500 rpm

DRIVETRAIN

Transmissions	6-speed manual, 4-speed automatic
Final-drive ratios	auto: 2.73:1 or 3.15:1; manual: 3.42:1, limited slip

DIMENSIONS

Wheelbase	105.7 in
Track, front/rear	62.1/60.7 in
Length/width/height	174.6/72.6/49.1 in
Ground clearance	5.0 in
Drag area, Cd (0.28) x frontal area (21.6 sq ft, est.)	6.05 sq ft
Curb weight	3250 lb
Weight distribution, F/R	51.0/49.0%
Curb weight per horsepower	8.13 lb
Fuel capacity	18.0 gal

CHASSIS/BODY

Type	full-length frame integral with the body
Body material	fiberglass-reinforced plastic

INTERIOR

SAE volume, front seat	52 cu ft
luggage	22 cu ft
Front-seat adjustments	fore-and-aft, seatback angle, front height, rear height
Restraint systems, front	manual 3-point belts, driver and passenger front airbags

SUSPENSION

Front	ind, unequal-length control arms, transverse plastic leaf spring, anti-roll bar
Rear	ind, unequal-length control arms with a toe-control link, transverse plastic leaf spring, anti-roll bar

STEERING

Type	rack-and-pinion with hydraulic power assist
Steering ratio	16.1:1
Turns lock-to-lock	2.6
Turning circle curb-to-curb	39.0 ft

BRAKES

Type	hydraulic with vacuum power assist and anti-lock control
Front	13.5 x 1.3-in vented disc
Rear	12.5 x 1.0-in vented disc

WHEELS AND TIRES

Wheel size	F: 8.5 x 18 in, R: 10.0 x 19 in
Wheel type	cast aluminum
Tires	Goodyear Eagle F1 GS or F1 SC; F: P245/40ZR-18, R: P285/35ZR-19

C/D-ESTIMATED PERFORMANCE (6-speed):

Zero to 60 mph	4.3 sec
Zero to 100 mph	10.0 sec
Standing 1/4-mile	12.7 sec @ 113 mph
Top speed (drag limited)	180 mph

PROJECTED FUEL ECONOMY

EPA city driving	18–19 mpg
EPA highway driving	25–28 mpg

compared with the LS1—and 400 pound-feet of torque at 4400 rpm. The LS2 is only five horsepower shy of the Z06's LS6 and makes just as much torque but at 400 fewer revs. Since the 2005 Corvette weighs no more than the C5, we estimate a 0-to-60-mph sprint of 4.3 seconds—a few 10ths quicker than the C5.

To stay ahead of the base car, the next Z06, due as a 2006 model, is rumored to have 500 horsepower, a dry-sump lubrication system, and a host of lightweight materials including aluminum side rails in place of the base car's steel ones.

One of the main focuses of the new car's development had nothing to do with thumping power, though. Chevy has its sights set on winning over buyers from high-end European sports cars, and it's an understatement to say the C5's dark and plasticky interior didn't stack up. So gone for 2005 are the shallow, chintzy cup holder, the finger-pinching center-stack compartment lid, and the interior door handles that looked wildly misaligned even when mounted correctly. We'll have to wait for a pro-duction sample to see how this all turns out. But the preproduction car we saw is a major improvement. The plastics don't glare at you as they did in the C5. The interior is brighter and appears larger—although it isn't. There are now two usable cup holders, map pockets in the doors, and a larger center console bin. There are even a few bits of real aluminum scattered about and seats with more thigh support. For the first time, the Corvette is available with a navigation system. As an added trick, the optional head-up display will record your maximum lateral acceleration from a driving session. Also, as on the Cadillac XLR, the Corvette will come standard with keyless unlocking and ignition.

Chevrolet isn't talking prices yet, but figure on a modest increase. The targa should start at about $45,000, the convertible at about $52,000.

Those expecting a clean-sheet new model might be disappointed by the C6. But at those prices and with thoughtful upgrades of virtually all the C5's weak points, the Corvette is now a better performance-car bargain than ever. ∎

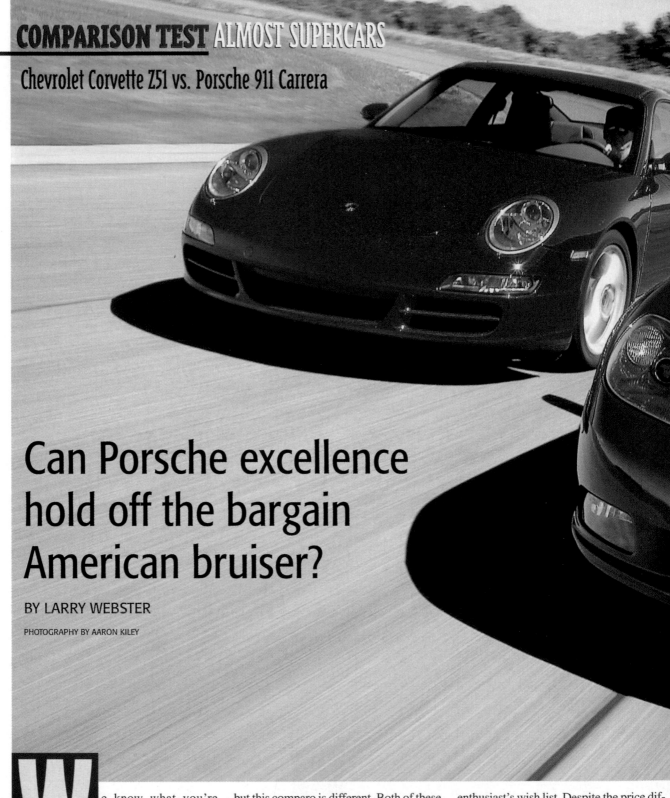

COMPARISON TEST ALMOST SUPERCARS

Chevrolet Corvette Z51 vs. Porsche 911 Carrera

Can Porsche excellence hold off the bargain American bruiser?

BY LARRY WEBSTER

PHOTOGRAPHY BY AARON KILEY

We know what you're thinking: This is not a fair fight. In one corner, there's the American value-packed brute, the $44,245 Corvette. And in the other, a high-priced *über*-coupe, Porsche's latest 911 (code-named 997), which costs a stunning $70,065.

Pitting cars with such wildly unequal prices (the 911 costs *58 percent more* than the Corvette) is not our standard practice,

but this comparo is different. Both of these are fantastically fast sports cars that are almost quick enough to be ranked as supercars but have prices that make them somewhat accessible. And whether they're used for commuting to work in reasonable comfort or getting your g-jollies at the track, these cars can do both jobs. Plus, they're new or, shall we say, extensively updated for 2005. These two legendary models both have an illustrious racing heritage, and they have at some point graced every

enthusiast's wish list. Despite the price difference, they have competed against each other numerous times in these pages (see sidebar).

And to be frank, we needed some real competition to put up against the Vette. Only the $48,995 BMW M3 is even close in performance and price. But the M3's back seat makes it a different kind of car, and even with a sultry 333-hp inline-six, its firepower wouldn't be adequate.

So the task fell to Zuffenhausen's fran-

chise player, the 911. For 2005, a freer-breathing intake system yielded six more ponies from the 3.6-liter aluminum flat-six. The total now stands at 321, with torque the same, at 273 pound-feet. That's 12 fewer horses than the M3 has, but the 911 weighs about 200 fewer pounds.

Thanks to wider fender flares, the 911 has a slightly increased track front and rear. The combination of a front-strut and rear-multilink suspension carries over, but the development process has continued, and

the entire system has been tweaked for the usual claims of a smoother ride and tighter handling.

There's a new interior, there are 18-inch wheels and tires, and finally, Porsche has gone back to the more upright head-light housings that we liked so much in previous models. It's a typical array of detail improvements that Porsche says add up to a major step forward. For the 911's sake, we hope so, because the Vette looks awfully strong.

Although the Vette, too, is an evolutionary version, its engine room received a serious bump. The aluminum V-8 is not only larger (5.7 to 6.0 liters) but also has a thumping 400 horses and 400 pound-feet of torque. The previous Vette had 50 fewer horses and 25 fewer pound-feet of torque when coupled to the six-speed manual gearbox.

The Corvette also gets a host of chassis changes, new bodywork, a new interior, and finally, such features as a navigation

system and heated seats. For a car so capable, the base price of $44,245 is a genuine bargain. Ours came with the $1495 Z51 suspension package that offers shorter transmission ratios, grippier tires, bigger brakes, and a transmission-oil cooler. It's the track hound of the Corvette lineup. In addition, $8500 worth of nonperformance options brought it to a grand total of $54,240.

The 911 arrived with a navigation system, bixenon headlights, a Bose stereo system, and a few other options, for $76,195.

As a couple of advertised do-everything sports cars, we put them through our usual battery of performance tests, along with 500 miles of highway and back-road driving, and since these cars are meant for

Vehicle		Chevrolet Corvette Z51	Porsche 911 Carrera
base price/ price as tested		**$44,245/** **$54,240**	$70,065/ $76,195
dimensions, in	length	174.6	175.6
	width	72.6	71.2
	height	49.1	51.6
	wheelbase	105.7	92.5
	track, front/rear	62.1/60.7	58.5/60.4
weight, pounds		3288	**3253**
weight distribution, % front/rear		52.1/47.9	38.4/61.6
fuel tank, gallons		18.0	16.9
recommended octane rating		93	91
interior volume, cu ft	front	52	48
	rear	–	**16**
	trunk	22	5
Best in test.			

the occasional romp at the track and we weren't popping for tires, we spent a day lapping 1.9-mile GingerMan Raceway in South Haven, Michigan.

Don't rush off to the results chart just yet. We made an adjustment to our ballot that needs explaining. It's an attempt to rectify the price discrepancy between these cars.

Our ballot has 21 categories that are worth a varying number of points, from a minimum of five to a maximum of 25. Drivers rate the cars in most categories, and others are calculated from dimensions or test results; then we average the scores and total the points. The car with the highest total wins. In our usual comparison tests, drivers can award a maximum of 10 points in the value category. But as

we noted, the Porsche's base price is 58 percent greater than the Chevrolet's—in a typical comparo the difference is closer to 15 percent. So for this test, the value category has a maximum of 20 points.

Considering that a perfect score in every category would be more than 200 points, this is a small change. But it's one that allowed voters to better consider each car's cost.

So, anyway, enough about points, here's how things played out.

Second Place
Porsche 911 Carrera

The 911's classic, time-weathered shape has never looked better. The wider fenders give a beefy, more purposeful look that complements the silhouette. And the

packaging benefits of the rear-engine layout are as handy as ever. For the first time, the 911 is longer than the Corvette. And the Porsche, at least, still has room for a couple of kids in the back seats.

So when it comes to handling, which is better, an engine in front or in back? For racing, the answer is neither—the mid-engine design is clearly better, as demonstrated by every purpose-built race car. But what about street cars that offer at least some practicality?

We're not going to answer that one because, well, there is no simple answer. Here, both of these cars are fantastic curve carvers. On the street, though, the nod goes to the 911.

We never found a patch of road that gave us even a whiff of that "Oh, %#$@!"

feeling that precedes some type of mid-corner correction or wheel sawing. Editor-at-large Pat Bedard calls this "path accuracy." At speed, how accurately can you place the car? With the 911, the answer is in fractions of an inch; with the Vette, it's in inches. This feeling likely is why the 911 went through the cones of our lane-change test 1.1 mph faster than the Vette. You can plant this car anywhere.

Although we were initially skeptical of the 911's variable-ratio steering, we're believers now. The ratio quickens the farther you turn the wheel, but you don't notice it. The effort is light, but the steering is wonderfully accurate.

Bumps have no effect on trajectory. The suspension is nicely supple and not the least bit floaty. It's a lot like the sus-

2 Porsche 911 Carrera

Highs: Telepathic steering and brake feel, an engine that sounds as good as it performs, you cannot upset this chassis.

Lows: Raising the seat via the manual adjuster tilts it forward, sticker shock.

The Verdict: Deserves to be lusted after.

penders of the BMW 3-series that we like so much. The 911 suspension is stiff enough to keep the chassis movements to a minimum and communicate irregularities to the driver but also resilient enough to absorb bumps and cushion blows. The 911 pulled 0.97 g on the skidpad, a tick less than the Vette's 0.98, but in every subjective handling category except one, the 911 outscored the Vette.

It also trailed the Vette in every speed contest except top-gear acceleration, where the Vette's hugely tall top gear puts the Chevy at a disadvantage. You have to grin and bear the gut-wrenching, axle-hopping launch to make the Porsche go its quickest, but the 911 seems to outperform its spec sheet. The power-to-weight ratio is 23 percent poorer than the Vette's, but the 911's rear weight bias keeps things close until speeds rise. At 60 mph, the

Powertrain		Chevrolet Corvette Z51	Porsche 911 Carrera	
engine	type	pushrod 16-valve V-8	DOHC 24-valve flat-6	
	displacement, cu in (cc)	364 (5967)	219 (3596)	
	power, bhp @ rpm	**400 @ 6000**	321 @ 6800	
	torque, lb-ft @ rpm	**400 @ 4400**	273 @ 4250	
	redline, rpm	6500	7200	
	lb per bhp	**8.2**	10.1	
driveline	transmission	6-sp man	6-sp man	
	driven wheels	rear	rear	
	gear ratios:1	2.97, 2.07, 1.43, 1.00, 0.71, 0.57	3.91, 2.32, 1.61, 1.28, 1.08, 0.88	
	axle ratio:1	3.42	3.44	
	mph/1000 rpm	7.6, 10.9, 15.8, 22.5, 31.8, 39.6	5.7, 9.5, 13.7, 17.3, 20.5, 25.1	
C/D test results / acceleration, seconds	0–60 mph	**4.1**	4.3	4.2
	0–100 mph	**9.6**	10.5	10.1
	0–150 mph	**25.0**	28.5	26.8
	¼-mile @ mph	**12.6 @ 114**	12.8 @ 109	12.7 @ 112
	rolling 5–60 mph	**5.1**	5.3	5.2
top-gear	30–50 mph	10.3	**7.6**	9.0
	50–70 mph	9.6	**7.9**	8.8
	top speed, mph	**186** (drag limited, mfr's claim)	181 (redline limited)	184
sound level, dBA	idle	60	**52**	56
	full-throttle	86	**83**	85
	70-mph cruise	74	76	75
fuel economy, mpg	EPA city	19	19	19
	EPA highway	28	26	27
	C/D 500-mile trip	18	17	18
Best in test.				Test Avg

Chassis		Chevrolet Corvette Z51	Porsche 911 Carrera	
front suspension		control arms, leaf spring, anti-roll bar	strut, coil springs, anti-roll bar	
rear suspension		control arms, leaf spring, anti-roll bar	multilink, coil springs, anti-roll bar	
front brakes		vented disc	vented disc	
rear brakes		vented disc	vented disc	
anti-lock control		yes	yes	
stability control		yes	yes	
tires		Goodyear Eagle F1 Supercar EMT; F: P245/40ZR-18 88Y, R: P285/35ZR-19 90Y	Michelin Pilot Sport PS2; F: 235/40ZR-18 91Y, R: 265/40ZR-18 101Y	
C/D test results	braking, 70–0, feet	164	**150**	*157*
	roadholding, 300-foot skidpad, g	**0.98**	0.97	*0.98*
	lane change, mph	66.8	**67.9**	*67.4*
Best in test.				*Test Avg*

Porsche's 4.3-second time is only 0.2 second slower than the Vette's, but at 150, the gap is 3.5 seconds.

The 911, therefore, needed a major handling advantage to outrun the Vette at GingerMan. No such trump card arose. Like most recent 911s, this one predominantly understeers, so in GingerMan's long corners, we had to wait seemingly forever to put the power down and accelerate out of the turns. The 911's best lap time of 1:37.95 was 2.3 seconds slower than the Vette's. That's an eternity in road racing.

Still, we love this Porsche. It has a visceral attitude that's been softened only enough so the car is perfectly livable. We'd need just one hand to count the things we'd change, and the manual seat-height adjuster that tilts the seat as it rises would be *numero dos*.

Numero uno is the price. Would we pay an extra five grand, over the Corvette, for the 911? That's a no-brainer; absolutely. Fifteen? Probably, but we'd have to think about it. Twenty? Well, you already know our answer: no.

First Place
Chevrolet Corvette Z51

We never thought this would be such a close match. After our first test of the C6 Corvette and before we'd piloted the new 911, we figured the Porsche was a mackerel, the Chevy a barracuda. But the Vette won by one measly point.

We even managed to wring a couple of 10ths out of the Vette's already stellar acceleration times. Chevy's sportster knifed to 60 mph in a scant 4.1 seconds, a couple 10ths quicker than the 2005 yellow car we tested in September. This red car was a little slower in top-gear acceleration tests, so we don't think it was a particularly strong example. Or maybe we simply got better at launching it.

It's far from a stoplight special, though. "Very nice highway car—smooth, quiet, refined. At 80 mph, I can barely hear the engine. Plus, I could easily get comfortable in the new, attractive interior," wrote one tester.

But Chevy hasn't removed all the Vette's traditional character. This is still a brute. For one, you look out over a long, wide hood. Although the Corvette is an inch shorter than the 911, ask anyone which is longer, and no one will get it right. Between the two, we all preferred the more expansive view out the 911.

You can't argue with the Vette's capabilities, though. On back roads, it can pull

December 1981

23 Years of Going Nose to Nose

We have put a 911 against a Corvette five times on these pages. Two of these encounters were multicar comparos, and three were head-to-heads. The first was in December 1981, when we pitted four sports cars against the De Lorean. Even then, the 911's as-tested price of $34,165 seemed audacious when compared with the $19,000 Vette. The horsepower numbers seem puny by today's weaponry standards: 172 for the Porsche and 190 for the Chevy. We didn't pick a winner or rank them, but it was clear the 911 easily had the Vette covered.

Fast-forward to September 1988, and the tide had shifted. Against the 214-hp 911 Club Sport, the 245-hp Corvette Z51 fell behind in acceleration tests but stormed ahead on the race and autocross courses. It was also about 15 grand cheaper, and it won.

Two years later, in a five-car roundup [September 1990], a $59,795, 375-hp ZR-1, dubbed the "Corvette from Hell," finished a hellish third, one spot behind the $80,257, 247-hp 911. Advantage Porsche.

And then a funny thing happened. In April 1991, the ZR-1 went head-to-head with the most powerful 911 of the day, the $105,191, 315-hp turbo model. It should've been a Porsche rout, but it wasn't—the Vette prevailed, due largely to a better-sorted suspension.

The next meeting came in May 1998. The 911 was strong for that meeting, besting the Vette to 60 mph and on the road course. But it wasn't enough to overcome the 30-grand price premium, and the Vette prevailed.

Do Porsche guys care that the score is now four to two for the Vette? Probably not. —LW

May 1998

1 Chevrolet Corvette Z51

Highs: Performance that puts most sports cars on the trailer, surprising comfort and value.

Lows: We'd give up some cush for more road feel and a throatier engine note.

The Verdict: Still a great car, but it's not the wunderkind we first thought it was.

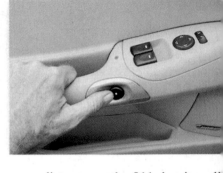

some distance on the 911, but it really makes you work for it. Two comments from the test-driver logbook: "The 911 doesn't throw you around nearly as much as the Vette over bumpy curves, and it's noticeably more stable." And this: "With the Vette, you have to tell yourself it's going to stay glued to the road, but in the 911, there's no need to wonder." On the smooth racetrack, up-and-down motions were still present and the chassis moved around a lot more than we expected. Plus, as in the 911, it was a little tricky to feed in power while coming off the turns, but for a different reason. Where the 911 slid its front tires, the Corvette was a little too eager to fishtail.

But that was the Vette's only vice, and in some ways it was an advantage. GingerMan has a lot of long, gradual curves, and if the Vette started to drift wide of the intended arc, a little added power could rotate the car back on line. We couldn't do that in the Porsche. And if we hung out the tail a little too far, it took only a quick dose of countersteering to put the car straight. The brakes, like those on the Porsche, didn't exhibit any fade during our five-lap sessions.

There is, however, a numbness to the chassis that was especially apparent when

compared with the Porsche, and that cost the Vette some points. The Chevy can be driven extremely quickly, but it doesn't inspire the same confidence as the Porsche. Although both these cars ride quite well, the Vette feels a little less buttoned down. It could use more precision and perhaps stiffer shocks.

The difference was most noticeable while braking. Stomp on the middle pedal in the Vette, and it practically stands on its nose, whereas the Porsche squats hard. The 911 stopped from 70 in only 150 feet, 14 fewer than the Corvette.

True, that difference is due largely to the Porsche's rear-weight bias, but taken as a complete car, the 911 has a tick more sharpness. The Vette's steering is lifeless in comparison to the 911's. Plus, Chevy could have done better with the shifter. The throws are short, but it's stiff, and it balks every once in a while at a gearchange. It's the opposite of the Porsche's precise and easy-moving rod.

We're talking nuances here; the difference in most categories amounted to only a point. The 911's added feel and precision must be what the extra money buys you, because despite the much lower price, the Vette still has more features, such as power seats, adjustable lumbar and side-bolster supports, and a nifty head-up readout showing lateral acceleration.

In the end, though, it was the Vette's outstanding value that carried the day, as it scored 20 points in that category to the 911's 15. It was a deficit the Porsche almost, but not quite, surmounted. As we've said before, for the money, there isn't a better sports car around. ■

Results

		Chevrolet Corvette Z51	Porsche 911 Carrera
vehicle	driver comfort (10)	10	9
	front-seat space* (10)	10	8
	ergonomics (10)	9	9
	trunk space* (5)	5	5
	features/amenities* (10)	10	8
	fit and finish (10)	9	10
	styling (10)	9	9
	value (20)	20	15
	total (85)	82	73
powertrain	engine output* (10)	10	8
	performance* (10)	10	8
	throttle response (10)	10	10
	engine NVH (10)	8	10
	transmission (10)	8	10
	total (50)	46	46
chassis	performance* (10)	9	10
	steering feel (10)	8	10
	brake feel (10)	9	10
	on-road handling (10)	9	10
	race-track handling (10)	9	9
	ride (10)	9	10
	total (60)	53	59
	gotta-have-it factor (25)	23	24
	fun to drive (25)	22	23
	grand total (245)	226	225
	finishing order	1	2

*These objective scores are calculated from the vehicles' dimensions, capacities, and/or test results. **Best in test.**

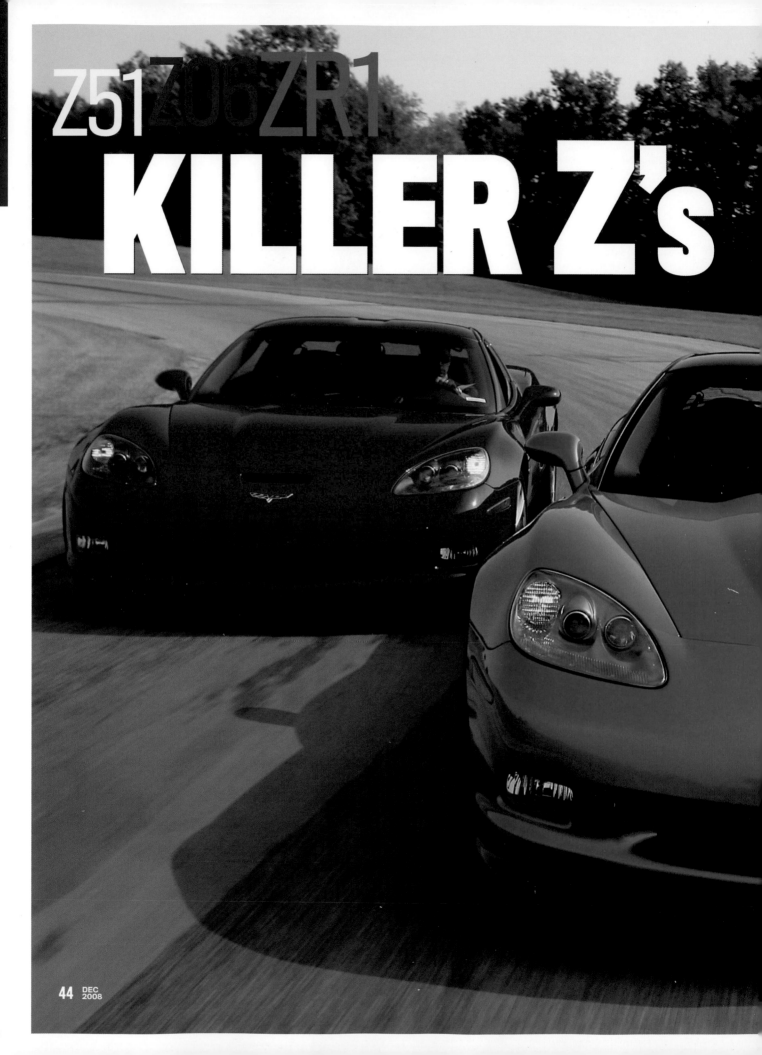

Z51 Z06 ZR1

KILLER Z's

THE ZR1 IS THE FASTEST
AND MOST EXPENSIVE
PRODUCTION CORVETTE EVER.
SO HOW DOES IT STACK UP
AGAINST ITS STABLEMATES?

BY MARK GILLIES
PHOTOGRAPHY BY RICH CHENET

Z51 Z06 ZR1

The glory days of the Corvette have generally coincided with the availability of an alphanumeric soup of engine and equipment packages. Go back to the 1960s and early '70s, and all sorts of near mythical combinations show up, with the LT1, L88, LS6, ZR-1, and Z06 being the most notable. Contrast that with the Vette's Dark Ages between the OPEC oil crisis and the introduction of the fourth-generation Corvette, the C4, in 1984, when the options lists were limited to some slightly more powerful engines and sportier suspensions.

The C4 and the subsequent C5 marked a return to form—and evocative alphanumerics associated with performance again appeared on the options lists. The 375-hp ZR-1 model debuted in 1990, though it was pricey—nearly double the sticker of a base 245-hp coupe. A Z51 suspension package was also available through the C4's (overly long) 13-year life. There was no ZR-1 for the 1997–2004 C5, but the Z06 performance model, latterly with 405 horsepower, commanded a premium of less than 20 percent over a base Corvette.

With the sixth-generation car, the C6, what's old is new again. Introduced in 2005, the C6 has now spawned Z06 and ZR1 variants, while the Z51 suspension-option remains. The cynical might suggest that the $105,000 ZR1 merely represents a serious profit center for GM, but the other view is that this 638-hp supercar reflects confidence in the Corvette brand and in Chevrolet's ability to engineer a car deserving such a price tag.

To see where the ZR1 (now hyphenless, kids!) stacks up, we decided to compare it with its stablemates. One could argue that we should be pitting the ZR1 against a Porsche 911 Turbo, but we reckon a 911 Turbo buyer is no more likely to cross-shop a ZR1 than a Yankees fan is to buy season tickets to the Red Sox. We think it's better to know what the ZR1 offers—if anything—beyond the Z06 and the regular coupe.

SPOT THE DIFFERENCES

With the cars lined up alongside each other, all our drivers made the same observation: The base yellow Corvette coupe, which ordinarily stands out on the road like a tiger in a room full of domestic cats, seems a little dowdy.

The Z06 and ZR1 look more taut and chiseled, thanks to wider front and rear

BIG, BIGGER, BIGGEST

The Z51's front brake discs (above) are 13.4 inches in diameter. The red Z06's are 14.0 inches, and the blue ZR1's are a massive 15.5.

C/D RESULTS BEST IN TEST	PRICE ($)		DIMENSIONS (inches)						WEIGHT			FUEL TANK (gal)	OCTANE RATING	INTERIOR VOL (cu ft)	
*EST VEHICLE	BASE	AS TESTED	LENGTH	WIDTH	HEIGHT	WHEEL-BASE	FRONT TRACK	REAR TRACK	CURB (lb)	% FRONT	% REAR			FRONT	TRUNK
CHEVROLET CORVETTE Z51	$49,590	$63,940	174.6	72.6	49.0	105.7	62.1	60.7	3273	51.8	48.2	18.0	91	52	22
CHEVROLET CORVETTE Z06	$73,255	$83,515	175.6	75.9	49.0	105.7	63.5	62.5	3210	50.4	49.6	18.0	91	52	22
CHEVROLET CORVETTE ZR1	$105,000	$117,750	176.2	75.9	49.0	105.7	63.5	62.5	3350	51.6	48.4	18.0	91	52	22

fenders, more-aggressive front fascias, and a profusion of slats and scoops that channel cool air and exhaust heat. The ZR1 adds sills, an air-dam extension, and a roof made of carbon fiber; a more prominent tail spoiler; somewhat tacky ZR1 badges; and a transparent panel in its carbon-fiber hood.

All three Corvettes roll on big rims: 18 inches up front and 19s in back on both the base and Z06 models. On the ZR1, there are 19s at the front and 20-inch rears. Large red brake calipers play peekaboo behind the wheels of the Z06, with blue ones on the ZR1. Chromed wheels are optional, ranging from $1850 to $2000, but this treatment seems a touch passé.

Inside, all our test cars came fully loaded and featured an optional full-leather treatment that is way classier than the standard vision in plastic. The nicely stitched leather, however, jars with some cheap plastic moldings in the center stack and a lame faux-carbon-fiber finish that runs through the cabin. That leather costs $8055 in the base car, $6515 in the Z06, and $10,000 in the ZR1, bundled with a navigation system and upscale audio. (The touch-screen nav system is a $1750 stand-alone option on the two other models.) There's a $55,410 difference in price between the ZR1 and the Z51, but interior changes are limited to a boost gauge in place of a battery-voltage meter, a 220-mph speedometer, and the ZR1 name emblazoned on the seatbacks and the gauge cluster.

ZR1 and Z06 buyers might not get a whole lot of extra interior equipment for their money, but they do get a lot more hardware. The base car comes with a 430-hp, 6.2-liter LS3 V-8 engine mated to a six-speed manual or automatic transmission. Our test car came with what we regard as the most significant option, the Z51 performance package, which incorporates stiffer springs and anti-roll bars, retuned shocks, shorter gear ratios, and larger-diameter brake rotors (13.4 inches in front and 13.0 inches in back, up from 12.8 and 12.0 inches). At $1695, the Z51 package looks like a value. We also like the $1195 dual-mode performance-exhaust system, which increases output from 430 horsepower and 424 pound-feet of torque to 436 and 428, respectively. A base Corvette coupe equipped with the Z51 package and exhaust system would run $50,785, but Chevy saddled our test car with another $13,155 of options.

For $23,655 above the cost of our Z51 test car, the Z06 adds plenty of performance-enhancing equipment. The LS7 engine uses a different block than the LS3 and displaces 7.0 liters. With the aid of light-weight titanium valves and connecting rods, it revs to 7000 rpm, 500 more than

FAST, FASTER, FASTEST

The yellow Z51 coupe was a ball around Grattan raceway but was 2.1 seconds off the pace of the red Z06. The blue ZR1 was a further 2.1 seconds quicker.

Z51 Z06 ZR1

the LS3. It uses a race-type dry-sump oiling system compared with the LS3's wet sump. This engine makes a stout 505 horsepower and 470 pound-feet of torque.

To handle the increased power and torque, the Z06's clutch, transmission, and half-shafts have been beefed up. The frame is aluminum instead of steel, and there are cast suspension pieces in place of welded items. There's even a magnesium front cradle instead of aluminum to save weight and add strength. The suspension design is carried over from the base car, with stiffer springs and anti-roll bars. The brakes are uprated, with 14.0-inch-diameter front and 13.4-inch rear rotors and six-piston front and four-piston rear calipers.

The ZR1 costs $31,745 more than the Z06. Like that car, the main news is under the hood. The supercharged 6.2-liter LS9 engine is based on the LS3 but with many changes. It has a forged steel crankshaft, titanium connecting rods, a dry-sump oil system, and hollow-stem exhaust valves. Titanium is also used for the intake valves. An Eaton R2300 supercharger and Behr intercooler force fuel and air into the engine, resulting in 638 horsepower and 604 pound-feet of torque.

To cope with the power, a two-disc clutch is fitted, and the gearbox and rear axle have been further strengthened. The gear ratios are closer than those of the Z06. The ZR1's suspension is shared, for the most part, with the two other models, although the fitment of magnetorheological variable-damping shocks allows for a softer ride than the Z06's. For the first time, a Corvette is equipped with carbon-

C/D RESULTS / BEST IN TEST — CHASSIS	SUSPENSION FRONT	SUSPENSION REAR	BRAKES FRONT	BRAKES REAR	ANTI-LOCK CONTROL	STABILITY CONTROL	TIRES	BRAKING 70–0 MPH (ft)	ROADHOLDING 300-FT-DIA SKIDPAD (g)	LANE CHANGE (mph)
CHEVROLET CORVETTE Z51	control arms, leaf spring, anti-roll bar	control arms, leaf spring, anti-roll bar	13.4-inch drilled, vented disc	13.0-inch drilled, vented disc	yes	yes	Goodyear Eagle F1 Supercar EMT; F: P245/40ZR-18 (88Y), R: P285/35ZR-19 (90Y)	152	0.99	65.1
CHEVROLET CORVETTE Z06	control arms, leaf spring, anti-roll bar	control arms, leaf spring, anti-roll bar	14.0-inch drilled, vented disc	13.4-inch drilled, vented disc	yes	yes	Goodyear Eagle F1 Supercar EMT; F: P275/35ZR-18 (87Y), R: P325/30ZR-19 (94Y)	150	1.03	67.5
CHEVROLET CORVETTE ZR1	control arms, leaf spring, anti-roll bar	control arms, leaf spring, anti-roll bar	15.5-inch drilled, vented ceramic disc	15.0-inch drilled, vented ceramic disc	yes	yes	Michelin Pilot Sport PS2 ZP; F: P285/30ZR-19 (87Y), R: P335/25ZR-20 (94Y)	142	1.07	67.5
							TEST AVERAGE	148	1.03	66.7

BEST IN TEST / **C/D* EST / *C/D* RESULTS — POWERTRAIN	ENGINE: POWER BHP @ RPM	ENGINE: TORQUE LB-FT @ RPM	REDLINE (rpm)	LB PER BHP	DRIVELINE: TRANSMISSION	DRIVEN WHEELS	GEAR RATIOS:1	AXLE RATIO:1	MPH/1000 RPM	ACCELERATION (seconds) MPH 0–60	0–100	0–150	¼-MILE @ MPH	ROLLING 5–60 MPH	TOP GEAR MPH 30–50	50–70	TOP SPEED (mph)	SOUND LEVEL (dBA) IDLE	FULL THROTTLE	70-MPH CRUISE	FUEL (mpg) EPA CITY	EPA HWY	350 MILES
CHEVROLET CORVETTE Z51 pushrod 16-valve V-8 376 cu in (6162cc)	436 @ 5900	428 @ 4600	6500	7.5	6-sp man	rear	2.97, 2.07, 1.43, 1.00, 0.71, 0.57	3.42	7.6, 10.9, 15.8, 22.6, 31.9, 39.7	4.1	9.0	22.2	12.4 @ 117	4.5	8.9	8.3	186 (drag ltd, mfr's claim)	60	91	79	16	26	25
CHEVROLET CORVETTE Z06 pushrod 16-valve V-8 428 cu in (7008cc)	505 @ 6300	470 @ 4800	7000	6.4	6-sp man	rear	2.66, 1.78, 1.30, 1.00, 0.74, 0.50	3.42	8.4, 12.6, 17.2, 22.4, 30.3, 44.8	3.6	8.3	17.3	11.7 @ 124	4.1	9.3	9.3	198 (drag ltd, mfr's claim)	60	92	76	15	24	20
CHEVROLET CORVETTE ZR1 supercharged pushrod 16-valve V-8 376 cu in (6162cc)	638 @ 6500	604 @ 3800	6500	5.3	6-sp man	rear	2.29, 1.61, 1.21, 1.00, 0.81, 0.67	3.42	9.8, 13.9, 18.5, 22.4, 27.7, 33.5	3.4	7.6	16.4	11.5 @ 128	4.0	6.2	5.1	205 (drag ltd, mfr's claim)	61	97	80	14	20	12
@CARANDDRIVER.COM CHECK OUT BEHIND-THE-SCENES PICTURES WE DIDN'T HAVE ROOM FOR.									TEST AVERAGE	3.7	8.3	18.6	11.9 @ 123	4.2	8.1	7.6	196	60	93	78	15	23	19

READY FOR TAKEOFF

At the track, the ZR1 caught air at well over 100 mph. Interior differences (below) are limited to a boost gauge in the ZR1 and seat motifs.

ceramic brakes—massive 15.5-inch-diameter front and 15.0-inch rear Brembo rotors. They're a slightly smaller version of the brakes used on the Bugatti Veyron.

TEST TIMES

All three Corvettes are spectacularly fast. The base model goes from 0 to 60 mph in 4.1 seconds and hits 100 mph in 9.0 seconds. The Z06 needs just 3.6 and 8.3 seconds for the same tasks, while the ZR1 hits 60 mph in 3.4 seconds and 100 mph in a stellar 7.6 seconds. That 100-mph time betters the likes of the Nissan GT-R, Porsche 911 Turbo, and Ferrari F430.

The 30-to-50 and 50-to-70-mph top-gear acceleration times are impressive, as is skidpad grip: 0.99 g for the coupe, rising to 1.07 g for the ZR1, which also has the best braking of any production car we have ever tested—it needed just 142 feet to slow from 70 mph to a standstill. The base car managed 152 feet (better than the last 911 Turbo we tested), and the Z06 took 150 feet.

ROAD WARRIORS

The base coupe is the most livable of the three. The highway ride is surprisingly supple, tire noise is relatively muted—except for some intrusive slap over expansion joints—and the engine hums away at 2000 rpm at 80 mph. We even managed to average 25 mpg during our test in the coupe, close to the EPA-highway figure of 26 mpg. That's astonishing when one considers that the car spent an afternoon being thrown roughly around Grattan Raceway Park in western Michigan.

On bumpy back roads, the Corvette was very composed, had tons of grip, and ate up the straightaways while being perfectly composed under braking. It sounds terrific, too, bellowing hard under full throttle. The only weaknesses are steering that isn't particularly communicative, even if the weight and accuracy are first-class, and a notchy shifter.

The Z06 is almost too much car for regular roads. On the highway, the ride is quite compliant, but it gets choppy over high-frequency, small-amplitude ripples. Surprisingly, it's quieter than the base car at 70 mph, though the engine is more raucous under hard acceleration, when the V-8 snarls in a harsher, less mellifluous manner. The shifter still has a manly action but was a lot smoother than the base car's. An observed fuel economy of 20 mpg is impressive considering the Z06's capabilities.

Although the Z06 is even faster and grippier than the base car, it's not as easy to drive hard on bumpy back roads, darting here and there in the braking zones. It crashes hard over the most pockmarked surfaces, and the steering feels a little less linear and more aggressive on turn-in.

The ZR1 is a more civilized ride than the Z06, although one needs to make sure the adjustable shocks are set in "Tour." "Sport" is as firm as it is in the Z06, whereas the softer setting is almost as supple as the base car's. Highway cruising is more rowdy, however, thanks to the shorter gear ratios and the noise emitted by the giant tires. The ZR1 got a woeful 12-mpg average, although the car did spend an awful lot of its time lapping around Grattan. The attainable EPA highway number of 20 mpg is a lot more respectable.

The car tends to tramline, unlike the other models, which means the driver needs a firm hand on bumpy back roads. We rated the ZR1's steering as the most linear and involving of the three cars. The brakes are stellar, despite some initial pedal softness. Like the two other cars, there's a marked step in power at roughly 3000 rpm, except that there's simply more thrust in this car. The engine noise is sublime, a sonorous exhaust growl that swells in volume with revs, accompanied by blower whine that creates a V-8 symphony.

TRACK STARS

Let's get this straight: The seats in all three cars are unacceptable. They're okay for street use, but they just don't provide the lateral support needed on a track. We all found that our legs hurt after driving at Grattan because we had to use them to brace ourselves under hard cornering.

Otherwise, all three are weapons on the track. The base coupe is very good, with nicely predictable on-the-limit handling. It will run wide if the driver tries to dive-bomb into a corner on the brakes or with the throttle closed, but the attitude can be converted to neutrality and then to progressive oversteer with power.

The Z06 is 2.1 seconds faster per lap than the Z51 but is hairy at the limit. We've said it before, but the combination of light-switch oversteer, instant breakaway from the Goodyear tires, and a slight numbness in the steering makes for a ride that's like one of those giant roller coasters: alternately so scary and exhilarating that you're not sure whether you enjoyed the experience.

The ZR1 is a far more sanitary device, despite going 2.1 seconds faster per lap than the Z06. It feels softer than the Z06, which gives the driver more warning of incipient breakaway, and the Michelin tires are much more progressive when they relinquish grip. Plus, the steering has more feel, and the brakes could stop a run on Wall Street. At Grattan, it was about as good as a road car can get on a circuit.

VERDICT: A CORVETTE WINS!

The loser among these three is the Z06. In the past, we've given the car something of a free pass simply because it provides such stupendous performance for about $70,000. It is still a great value, but the Z51 and the ZR1 highlight its major fault, namely that it's really difficult to drive hard on a track, which is supposedly its raison d'être.

The base coupe is also a great value and mighty fine to drive, too. It is relatively comfortable on the highway, very practical, and really fast on road and track. Sure, the interior is Third World standard unless you order the $8000 optional leather package, but one can live with that for a base price of less than $50,000. As one test driver noted, "This is as much Corvette as I really need."

The ZR1 is a spectacular car. Yes, it has an interior that wouldn't pass muster in an $18,000 Hyundai let alone a $105,000 sports car, and it looks, well, like a Corvette (on steroids). But it is a great piece of work: faster, easier to drive at the limit, and more comfortable in daily use than the Z06. It is one of those rare cars, such as the Ferrari 430 Scuderia and the BMW M3, that make its driver look more heroic than reality suggests. To do that with a car that has such formidable performance is a rare feat. »

Z51 Z06 ZR1

GRATTAN RACEWAY • BELDING, MICHIGAN • 2.0 MILES

SPEED THROUGH TURN 11
ZR1: 91 mph
Z06: 95 mph
Z51: 91 mph
Katech Z06: 93 mph

LAP TIMES
ZR1: 1:24.9/84.8 mph
Z06: 1:27.0/82.8 mph
Z51: 1:29.1/80.8 mph
Katech Z06: 1:25.5/84.2 mph

PEAK SPEED
ZR1: 150 mph
Z06: 144 mph
Z51: 137 mph
Katech Z06: 148 mph

AVERAGE BRAKING G's
ZR1: 1.14 g
Z06: 0.98 g
Z51: 0.96 g
Katech Z06: 1.04 g

PEAK SPEED BETWEEN TURNS 9 AND 10
ZR1: 107 mph
Z06: 104 mph
Z51: 103 mph
Katech Z06: 103 mph

G's THROUGH TURN 3
ZR1: 1.23 g
Z06: 1.16 g
Z51: 0.99 g
Katech Z06: 1.11 g

PEAK SPEED BEFORE JUMP
ZR1: 105 mph
Z06: 99 mph
Z51: 97 mph
Katech Z06: 104 mph

The ZR1's grunt and great brakes gave it an edge around Grattan, as did the improved power-to-weight ratio and grip of the Katech car over the Z06. The Katech Z06 suffered over bumps such as the one between Turns 9 and 10. Speed before the jump was dependent on the exit from Turn 4.

THE CORVETTE FROM KATECH

On paper, the formula for the ClubSport Z06 from Clinton, Michigan–based Katech Performance sounds inviting. Take a Z06, remove 201 pounds, fit a double-adjustable coil-over suspension, add a Brembo brake kit, and install super-grippy Michelin Pilot Sport Cup tires. On the test track, it delivers: The Katech car was as fast from 0 to 60 mph as the ZR1 (3.4 seconds), and it hit 100 mph in 7.8 seconds. It beat all the Corvettes on the skidpad with 1.12 g of grip, owing to the tires. It looks pretty wicked, thanks to a subtle Katech body kit,

a carbon-fiber hood, and striking wheels, along with its lowered stance.

In the real world, there are a number of problems. It sounds amazing, although 99 decibels at wide-open throttle gets incredibly wearing after, oh, about five miles on the highway—as does the ride, which is race-car stiff.

One might think that its true métier would be the track, and up to a point, that's the case because it took 1.5 seconds off the Z06's lap time. But although the steering feel is more engaging than the Z06's, it's even twitchier at the limit, and the car gets knocked off line over the slightest bump.

Sure, it's nearly as fast as the ZR1 around the track, but this driver needed to take plenty of bravery pills before attempting a quick lap, whereas the ZR1 was actually much friendlier. And while you might think that the Katech route would end up being cheaper than the ZR1, it isn't. The base price for this one is an eye-popping $109,000. ●

First published in 2011 in the United States of America
by Filipacchi Publishing
1271 Avenue of the Americas
New York, NY 10020

Car and Driver is a registered trademark of Hachette Filipacchi Media U.S., Inc.

Jacket design
D'Mello + Felmus

Editor
Martin Padgett

Production
Lynn Scaglione and Annie Andres

ISBN-13: 978-1-936297-49-8

Library of Congress control number: 2010940273

Printed in China